COLLEGE TRANSFER
SUCCESS

THIRD EDITION

MAKING A SMOOTH TRANSITION

By Alyssa Bethel Williams, M.A. and Donna Dimsdale Housman, M.S.

Published by CPCC Press

www.cpccpress.com

Copyright © 2015 by CPCC Press, PO Box 35009, Charlotte, North Carolina 28235-5009

All rights reserved.

ISBN 10: 1-59494-079-7

ISBN 13: 978-1-59494-079-8

Book design by Cheree Moore, chereemooredesigns.com

Published and printed in the United States of America

For additional information you are invited to contact:

Alyssa Williams and Donna Housman

Central Piedmont Community College

PO Box 35009

Charlotte, N.C. 28235-5009

704.330.6357 or 704.330.4854

alyssa.williams@cpcc.edu

donna.housman@cpcc.edu

CPCC Press is a division of Central Piedmont Community College Services Corporation.

704.330.6731

www.cpccservicescorporation.com

TABLE OF CONTENTS

INTRODUCTION 1-5

UNIT 1 7-63

Section 1: Taking Personal Responsibility 8
Exercise 1.1A: 4 Steps to Getting Control of Your Time 14-17
Exercise 1.1B: My Critical Thinking Map 22
Exercise 1.1C: Academic Status and GPA 27
Section 2: Navigating College Systems & Support 28
Exercise 1.2A: Are You Ready for Online Learning? 34-36
Exercise 1.2B: Student Support 40
Section 3: Learning Strategies for Academic Success 42
Exercise 1.3: Academic Readiness Assessment 63

UNIT 2 65-103

Section 1: Self Assessment 66
Exercise 2.1A/Option A: Work Values Sorter 70
Exercise 2.1A/Option B: Discovering Your Values 71
Exercise 2.1B: Interest Profiler 74
Exercise 2.1C: Discovering Your Personality 75
Exercise 2.1D: Developing Your Skills 76-77
Section 2: Researching & Evaluating Your Career 78
Exercise 2.2: Career Research 81
Section 3: Deciding Your Career & Major 86
Exercise 2.3: Deciding Your Major 90
Section 4: Planning & Implementation 91
Exercise 2.4A: Career & Education Plan 100
Exercise 2.4B: Career & Education Goals 101
Exercise 2.4C: Action Plan 102

UNIT 3 105-163

Section 1: College Culture & Admissions 106
Exercise 3.1A: College Culture Evaluation 118-119
Exercise 3.1B: Transfer Admissions Plan 120-125
Section 2: Course Planning & Articulation Agreements 126
CAA Transfer Credit Appeal Procedure 141
Exercise 3.2: Academic Program Evaluation 144-146
Section 3: Paying for College 148
Exercise 3.3A: Financial Plan for College 158-160
Exercise 3.3B: Housing 161
Exercise 3.3C: Scholarship 162

UNIT 4 165-177

Making the Transition 166
Exercise 4.1: Making the Transition Reflection & Transfer Action Plan ... 176-177

APPENDIX 178-179

INDEX 180-182

ABOUT THE AUTHORS

ALYSSA BETHEL WILLIAMS, M.A., is a faculty member at Central Piedmont Community College in Charlotte, N.C. She has more than 22 years of experience as an instructor, advisor and trainer of adults in the public, private and community college sectors of higher education. Her areas of collegiate experience include leadership development, career counseling, new student orientation, academic advising, residence life, Greek affairs, judicial affairs, services for differently abled students and programming. She is a graduate of Tusculum College and received a Master of Arts degree in Student Development for Higher Education from Trinity University. In her current role, she is an instructor and Discipline Chair for Career Assessment and College Transfer Success, and teaches College Student Success and College Study Skills courses. Alyssa has also trained adults in the corporate arena on effective leadership, team building, group facilitation, diversity and conflict mediation and resolution.

DONNA HOUSMAN, M.S., is a faculty member at Central Piedmont Community College in Charlotte, N.C. She has over 25 years of experience in teaching and training adults in corporate, academic and public settings, focusing on leadership and management development, facilitation skills, self-awareness and team building. She is a graduate of Wake Forest University and has a Master of Science degree in Adult Education from Virginia Polytechnic Institute and State University. In her current role she teaches College Study Skills, Career Assessment, College Transfer Success and College Student Success. Her interests are also in improving students' readiness for online learning, incorporating global learning into her classroom, and ensuring that community college students are adequately prepared for university transfer. She previously taught English as a Second Language classes, providing civics-based ESL instruction for intermediate and advanced ESL students, and served as an instructor for ESL Fast Track Teacher Training.

ACKNOWLEDGMENTS

This textbook is a project that would not have been possible without the guidance, support, encouragement, feedback and contributions of many individuals. These individuals selflessly extended their valuable assistance in the preparation and completion of this project.

First, we are grateful to our students. Your commitment to your academic and career pursuits inspired us to pursue this project in a way that would have a significant impact on your educational goals. Our ultimate purpose is to provide you with the information and skills that will be a catalyst for your successful transfer to a four-year college or university.

We would like to acknowledge with appreciation the following individuals for your input, advice and support: Sara Baber, James Bass, Marquis Brown, Jordan Bullington, Erica AngaLay, Riley Ann Democko, Allen Lee Dowler Jr., Mark Helms, Connie Johnston, Paul Koehnke, Patty Martinez, Erin Phillips, Joy Scott, McKenna Smith, Owen Sutkowski, Alana Tarrano, Thomas Tillman, Jerome Walker, and the ACA Team: Laura Bazan, Juliet Laughlin, Jennifer Perkins and Linda Dunham. We sincerely appreciate your willingness to share your experience, insight and feedback. Your contributions were invaluable to this effort.

Finally, we would like to express our gratitude to the CPCC Services Corporation and CPCC Press: Quincy Foil White, Emma Reynolds and Amy Rogers, and to our designer Cheree Moore of Cheree Moore Designs. Your creativity, support and encouragement were essential to the development of this textbook. Thank you for being the catalyst through which we could express our vision. We are grateful to be a part of your team.

We hope this textbook will serve as a framework that will enable students to address and take responsibility for their transfer admission and degree completion at a four-year college or university. Our goal is to promote the ability of all students to embrace the integration of the academic and student support environments of a college to achieve successful degree completion and ensure readiness for their professional careers. Thanks to each of you for your contributions that have helped shape this textbook.

Alyssa Bethel Williams
Donna Dimsdale Housman

INTRODUCTION

CONGRATULATIONS on making the decision to continue your education after your community college experience is complete. You have made a wise decision and are following in the footsteps of close to half of the undergraduates in the United States.

"Nearly half of all students graduating with a four-year degree in the 2013-14 school year had some experience within a two-year institution. According to a report released in March 2015 by the National Student Clearinghouse Research Center, 46 percent of all students who completed a four-year degree had been enrolled at a two-year institution at some point in the past 10 years." (Inside Higher Ed, March 2015)

As a transfer student, your ultimate goal is to complete specific classes at the community college, such as your general education requirements or to complete an associate's degree, and then move on to your four-year university to get your bachelor's degree or higher. You may be getting the degree due to the requirements of the career you are entering or to have upward movement and more opportunities in your field. In fact, research shows the higher your level of education, the lower your unemployment and the higher your earnings will be.

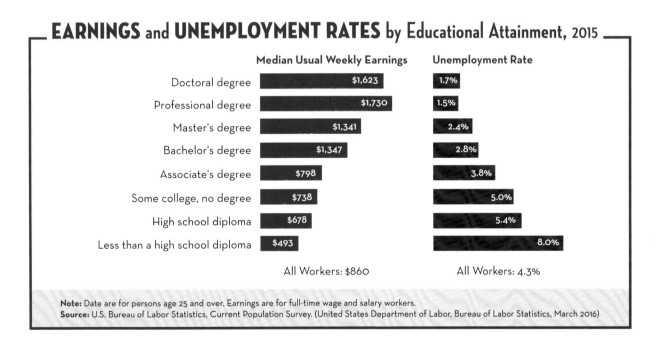

EARNINGS and UNEMPLOYMENT RATES by Educational Attainment, 2015

	Median Usual Weekly Earnings	Unemployment Rate
Doctoral degree	$1,623	1.7%
Professional degree	$1,730	1.5%
Master's degree	$1,341	2.4%
Bachelor's degree	$1,347	2.8%
Associate's degree	$798	3.8%
Some college, no degree	$738	5.0%
High school diploma	$678	5.4%
Less than a high school diploma	$493	8.0%
	All Workers: $860	All Workers: 4.3%

Note: Date are for persons age 25 and over. Earnings are for full-time wage and salary workers.
Source: U.S. Bureau of Labor Statistics, Current Population Survey. (United States Department of Labor, Bureau of Labor Statistics, March 2016)

Starting your bachelor's degree at the community college has many benefits:

➜ The cost of attending a community college is less expensive than universities.
➜ Classes are usually smaller and students can receive more individual attention.
➜ Students may be offered priority admissions to four-year colleges/universities based on agreements in their state.
➜ Great accessibility and flexibility allows students to live at home, work and save money.
➜ If necessary, students can overcome academic deficiencies and get better prepared for college-level work.

The bottom line: Many community college students are better prepared to go on to a four-year college or university after earning a two-year degree or after satisfying their general education requirements.

As a transfer student, there is not a "one size fits all" approach. You may be a recent high school graduate, a student with previous credits from another community college or university, a student coming from the military to complete your degree, or a high school student taking college classes. Don't worry! In this textbook we will answer many of your questions and go through a systematic process to help you with the successful transition to your university.

> "The information contained in this textbook is essential to navigating the transfer process. No matter where a student is on his or her path to a four-year degree, there are resources within this guide to *assist and support* that transition."
>
> — OWEN SUTKOWSKI, ED.D., DIRECTOR, TRANSFER RESOURCE CENTER & CAREER SERVICES, CPCC

The College Transfer Success textbook was created to assist students in their successful transfer from a community college to a four-year institution. It will provide information and strategies necessary to develop clear academic and professional goals beyond the community college experience. Topics include the Comprehensive Articulation Agreement (CAA), college culture, paying for college, course planning, student affairs, career exploration, researching information on four-year institutions, strategic planning, critical thinking, and communication skills for a successful academic transition.

Whatever your situation, this textbook will help you answer questions such as:

➔ What career will I choose and how do I choose my major?
➔ How do I know the best college to choose for my major?
➔ When and how do I start planning for transfer?
➔ What things do I need to consider to ensure a proper fit for me culturally, socially and academically?
➔ What are the admission requirements to the school?
➔ Will they accept the courses I have already taken for credit toward an advanced degree?
➔ What financial aid or scholarships might be available to me?

Transferring successfully from your community college will require you to answer these questions and many others. You will have the opportunity to consider what college will meet your personal, social, academic, financial and cultural needs, which brings us to the learning outcomes.

THE STUDENT LEARNING OUTCOMES ARE:

1. DEMONSTRATE THE BASIC SKILLS necessary to research four-year institutions, and develop a strategic plan for completing community college academic goals, including certificates, diplomas, and/or associate degrees.

2. DEMONSTRATE THE ABILITY TO IDENTIFY the rights and responsibilities of transfer students under the Comprehensive Articulation Agreement (CAA), including Universal General Education Transfer Component (UGETC) designated courses, the Transfer Assured Admissions Policy (TAAP), the CAA appeals process, and the university tuition surcharge.

3. DEVELOP A STRATEGIC PLAN for successfully transferring to a university and preparing for a new career.

4. EVALUATE LEARNING STRATEGIES, including note-taking, test-taking, information processing, time management, memorization techniques, and identify strategies for improvement.

5. IDENTIFY ESSENTIAL COLLEGE RESOURCES, including financial aid, advising, registration, tutoring, library services, computer labs and counseling services, and recognize the importance of these resources to student success.

6. IDENTIFY ESSENTIAL COLLEGE POLICIES and procedures, including academic integrity, such as avoiding plagiarism, calculating a GPA and maintaining satisfactory academic progress for financial aid eligibility and/or good academic standing.

Throughout the text we will address the Five Phases of College Transfer Success as well as address the learning outcomes. The five phases and the learning outcomes serve as a framework to guide us as we move through the transfer process.

PHASE 1 — Intro to College Life (Learning Outcome 4 & 6)

➜ Taking personal responsibility
➜ Navigating college systems and support
➜ Enhancing learning strategies for academic success

PHASE 2 — Self-Discovery and Career Exploration (Learning Outcome 3)

➜ Self-assessment
➜ Researching and evaluating your career
➜ Choosing your career and major
➜ Setting and implementing goals

PHASE 3 — Explore Your Best College Fit
(Learning Outcome 1, 2 & 5)

→ Understanding college culture
→ Exploring the best colleges for your career, major and individual needs
→ Exploring the cost of and sources available to help pay for college
→ Understanding transfer articulation agreements
→ Investigating academic program course planning and degree requirements
→ Creating an academic plan for the community college experience and university transfer

PHASE 4 — Your Transfer Admissions Plan
(Learning Outcome 3)

→ Researching admission requirements
→ Conducting college interviews/campus visits
→ Creating an admissions tracking system and timeline
→ Completing your transfer and financial aid applications

PHASE 5 — Making the Transition
(Learning Outcome 3)

→ Evaluating your university transfer options and accepting your final offer
→ Identifying and accessing resources to make the transfer transition successful

We hope this textbook will be a close companion as you work your way through the transfer process and that you feel more confident and ready to make the transition to a university after working through the decisions presented here.

"The *keys to a successful transfer* are knowledge and organization. This course will give you those tools and show you just how successful you can be! In the stressful time of trying to figure out my place in life, what I can offer my community, and which path to choose, this course has given me great assurance. Developing proper decision making skills, becoming familiar with resources used to find important information on specific colleges and figuring out annual costs, plus how financial aid can help, were some of the most beneficial lessons to me. The textbook provides a space to gather everything I have learned and organizes the information in a way that eliminates overwhelming questions and concerns. After the completion of this course I truly feel like I am ready to take on a four-year university at full speed and I now have the confidence to pursue all of my dreams."

— ALANNA TARRANO, CPCC STUDENT, SPRING 2016

INTRO TO COLLEGE LIFE

IN THIS UNIT:

→ Section 1: Taking Personal Responsibility

→ Section 2: Navigating College Systems & Support

→ Section 3: Learning Strategies for Academic Success

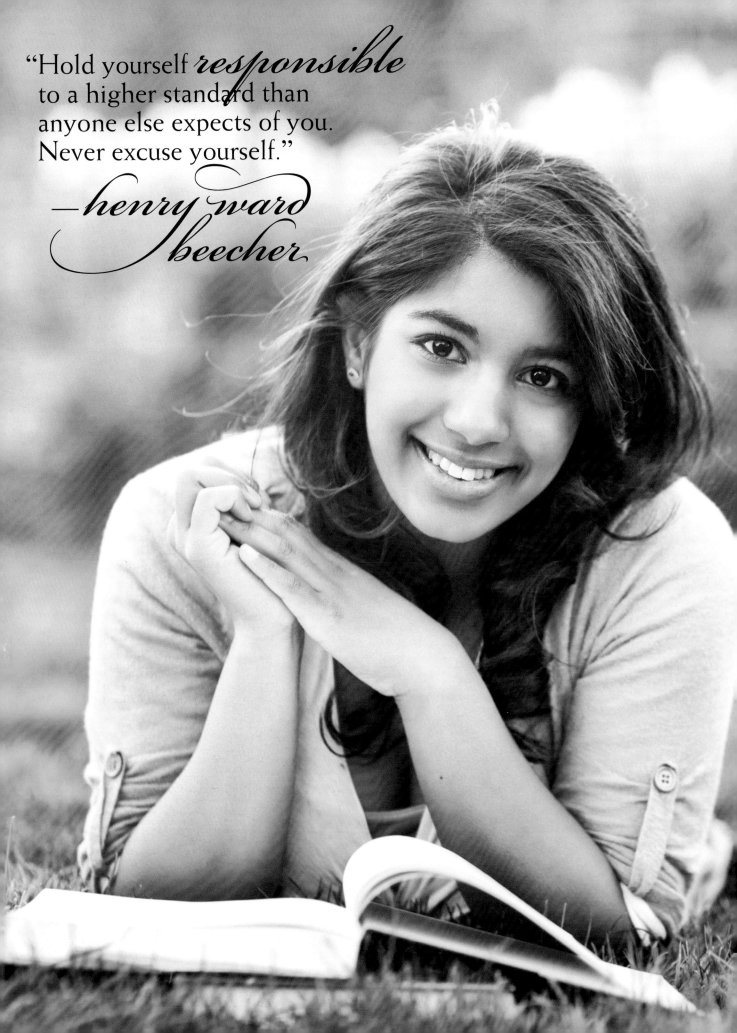

"Hold yourself *responsible* to a higher standard than anyone else expects of you. Never excuse yourself."

—henry ward beecher

SECTION 1 | TAKING PERSONAL RESPONSIBILITY

IN THIS SECTION:

→ Understand the Importance of
   Personal Responsibility

→ Learn Effective Time Management
   and Prioritization

→ Discover the Value of Critical Thinking
   and Decision Making

→ Define the Student Code of Conduct
   and Academic Integrity

SECTION 1 | TAKING PERSONAL RESPONSIBILITY

PERSONAL RESPONSIBILITY
SYSTEMS & SUPPORT
LEARNING STRATEGIES

Welcome to college! You are about to embark on one of the most exciting times of your life, one in which you will grow and develop as a person on your way to becoming a productive citizen in our society. College will be a different educational experience from what you have experienced up to this point in your life.

This first unit is called Intro to College Life. Here you will explore the foundational elements for being successful as you endeavor to obtain a holistic college education. In this unit you will learn:

→ more about the importance of PERSONAL RESPONSIBILITY;

→ how to navigate college SYSTEMS AND SUPPORT areas; and

→ how to ensure your academic success through effective LEARNING STRATEGIES.

PERSONAL RESPONSIBILITY

SYSTEMS & SUPPORT

LEARNING STRATEGIES

PERSONAL **RESPONSIBILITY**

At the core of your success as a college student and in life is your level of personal responsibility. It's when you take the ultimate onus for your academic and professional achievements, experiences and outcomes. Eduard C. Lindeman's five assumptions about adult learners are:

- → that they are motivated to learn as they experience needs and interests that learning will satisfy;
- → that their orientation to learning is life-centered;
- → that the richest source for the adult's learning is experience;
- → that adults have a deep need to direct themselves;
- → and that people's individual differences increase with age.

Lindeman's assumptions serve as an excellent foundation for the Six Key Attributes of Successful College Students.

- → Self-Awareness
- → Self-Motivation
- → Emotional Intelligence
- → Interdependence
- → Self-Efficacy
- → Accountability

Self-Awareness

Self-awareness is the capacity for introspection and the cognizance of one's own character, feelings, motives and desires. It is important you know yourself, your abilities and your limitations. Successful students are able to set high but realistic goals and take the appropriate level of risks. Self-awareness leads to effective self-direction.

Self-Motivation

Self-motivation is the inner strength that drives you to get things accomplished. There are two types: **INTRINSIC** (because you want to) is based on perceived or expected satisfaction. **EXTRINSIC** (because you have to) is based on the attainment of reward. It is essential to have personal drive, commitment, initiative and a positive attitude or fervor/perseverance to forge ahead in the wake of obstacles. To maintain your motivation, identify and improve your weaknesses. Hone and build on your strengths. Surround yourself with positive and supportive people. View obstacles, problems and challenges as opportunities for learning, growth and development.

Emotional Intelligence

Emotional intelligence is the ability to manage your emotions as they occur and evolve while in pursuit of your goals. It is developed and improved by learning and practicing new skills. Strong emotional intelligence will make it easier to form and maintain interpersonal relationships. It will also make is easier for students to adjust to the classroom and campus aspects of college life. It also helps students more effectively manage stress levels.

Interdependence

Interdependence is the ability to build a support system that will help you reach your academic endeavors. A support system will provide you constant feedback on how you are performing and areas that need improvement. Interdependence is a two-way street – you should be the same source of support for others.

Self-Efficacy

Self-efficacy is your own belief and confidence in your ability to accomplish what is necessary to bring goals to fruition. This requires a commitment to the direction of your learning, an ability to seek out resources for support and the desire to succeed. You must also be committed to life-long learning as you will find a need for valuable learning in every experience. Your desire for life-long learning will also cultivate a need for continued growth, development and success.

Accountability

Accountability is your ability to take ultimate ownership for your actions and outcomes. If along your journey in college you make a mistake or misstep, you take responsibility for and own it. This is a positive step toward resolution.

Students who lack personal responsibility often see themselves as victims, feel an inadequate ability to fulfill desired outcomes and lack the competence to motivate themselves. They are often poor managers of their time and procrastinate with carrying out tasks. These students also struggle to identify helpful resources and retreats rather than seeking support. They lack the ability to embrace change, try new ideas and take risks.

Situational REACTIONS

When faced with a challenging situation or a failed attempt at something, students who take personal responsibility respond with behaviors that promote future success. Students who evade taking responsibility tend to repeat the same responses and behaviors, resulting in the same failed outcomes in most situations.

THE RESPONSIBLE STUDENT	THE IRRESPONSIBLE STUDENT
REACTIONS	
Seeks to find solutions	Complains about the situation
Assumes accountability	Makes excuses
Takes action to find a resolution	Blames others or environmental circumstances
Embraces the notion of doing things differently	Repeats the same behavior
Turns obstacles/failures into motivation	Doubts him/her self
OUTCOMES	
Often experiences goal achievement and success	Rarely experiences goal achievement and success

TIME MANAGEMENT and Prioritizing

College life is exciting, but it can also be incredibly demanding. Effective time management is one of the common threads among most successful college students. It helps students get work done in a timely manner while excelling both inside and outside of the classroom.

Up to this point throughout your life, other people probably took some or all of the responsibility for keeping you organized. In school, teachers kept track of your work and monitored your performance. Your parents maintained your important records, made and arranged transportation to your appointments, made sure your homework got done and may have even kept your clothes clean. In college, the onus is on you. You now have to assume these responsibilities and more.

The skill of managing your time effectively while in college is a must. It is important to your success as a student. Effective time management is the conscious decision in which you decide what things are important in your life, then plan your time and life around these things. It is fundamentally the most important organizational skill

10 THINGS
YOU MUST STOP DOING TO BETTER MANAGE YOUR TIME

1. Showing up late
2. Showing up unprepared
3. Letting others deflect your focus
4. Saying yes to everyone
5. Convincing yourself that you don't need a system for organizing/planning your time
6. Forgetting to notify when you can't follow through
7. Being unrealistic about time commitments
8. Procrastinating
9. Trying to focus on doing too many things at one time/multitasking
10. Making excuses

you need to develop in order to be successful in college. It increases your productivity and helps decrease your stress level while promoting student success. Play a proactive role by knowing what your goals are, getting organized and planning in advance.

So, how well do you manage your time? Do you manage time...or does time manage you? For many of us, it seems as if we're always bouncing from one crisis to another. The purpose of this section is to help you improve your college life by learning how to better prioritize and balance your time.

BENEFITS OF Effective Time Management

➔ **It will help you to find balance**, decrease stress levels and gain a sense of inner peace. Your quality of life will improve as you begin to identify your limits and be unafraid to say "NO." You will also find yourself making fewer mistakes while freeing up more time for other things.

➔ **It promotes self-sufficiency** as you play a more proactive role of knowing what your goals are, getting organized, planning in advance, maintaining a calendar/planner and writing everything down in one place. Remember to be flexible and learn to expect the unexpected.

➔ **It aids in the achievement of your life goals**. Effective time management keeps you on task with your academic and career goals. You will find that it benefits all areas of your life as you prioritize what is important and what needs to get done.

TIPS FOR Effective Time Management

➔ Decide what tool works best for you, as an individual

➔ Create a schedule and plan your week

➔ Make a daily "TO DO" list and prioritize it

➔ Set goals that are specific, measureable, attainable, realistic and time focused

➔ Honor deadlines and avoid procrastinating

➔ Know your limits and don't be afraid to say "NO"

➔ Watch out for time gobblers (social media, TV, texting/phone)

➔ Always re-evaluate what is or is not working and how you can improve

It is also important to remember you are not meant to concentrate on one thing to the exclusion of all else. Your emphasis will probably shift somewhat over time. Someone finishing up a degree is likely to place extra importance on time spent alone for reading and writing. And as degrees are completed, your focus will probably shift somewhat. Make sure you give yourself time for relaxation, for exercise, for friends and for fun. These are critical parts of the "whole" person. And without taking care of ourselves, we do not have the energy we need to take care of the demands on our time.

EXERCISE 1.1A | **4 STEPS TO** GETTING CONTROL OF YOUR TIME

STEP 1 Self-Analysis

For one week, monitor how you spend your days. Write down everything you do every day for seven days, from the time you wake up until the time you go to bed. Include meals, class, work, study time/groups, phone calls, texting, time on social media, socializing with friends, sports/working out, watching TV, checking emails, daily travel time and exactly how long you spend doing each of these things. This will help you get a sense of your strengths and weaknesses in managing your time and to identify your time wasters. At the end of the week, crunch the numbers. Evaluate how well you spent your time. Take notice of patterns by answering the following questions.

1) ➔ How much time did you spend studying each day?

2) ➔ How long did you linger and chat with friends/family during each meal?

3) ➔ How much time each day did you spend checking social media, email, and texting?

4) ➔ What were the surprises?

5) ➔ When are your most productive times during the day?

6) ➔ Where did you waste time?

7) ➔ Did you tend to procrastinate?

8) ➔ What did you find yourself forgetting to do?

9) ➔ What did you spend the most time doing each day?

10) ➔ How would you rate your overall efficiency as a time manager on a scale of 1 (low) to 5 (high)?

STEP 2 Create Your Schedule

First, create your **"MASTER CALENDAR"** which should include important dates for the semester. Include due dates for projects, assignments, group presentations, papers and exam dates. The syllabi for all of your classes and the college's academic calendar will have this information. Also, include all of your important personal dates such as birthdays, anniversaries, religious holidays, special events or trips. You will need to combine both lists, note the dates that overlap and then decide which one will take precedence.

Next, create your **WEEKLY SCHEDULE**. Write out your fixed schedule: classes, part-time work hours, sports practice, etc. Then, refer to your "Master Calendar," and fill in the items most relevant to that week, such as when it is appropriate to work on projects, mandatory assignments for classes, prep for an upcoming test, pick up an anniversary gift and/or attend an event. Also, you should schedule at least two to three hours of study time for each hour you spend in class.

WEEKLY STUDENT CALENDAR OPTIONS

Test out using an electronic (Outlook, Yahoo, etc.) and a handheld calendar to decide your preference. Create a calendar for this academic semester using the course syllabus and create a **WEEKLY TO-DO** list. Your calender events must include this week's classes, homework assignments/project due dates, study groups, work schedule and family related events.

JAN

M	T	W	T	F	S	S
28	29	30	31	1	2	3
4	5	6	7	8	9	10
11	12	13	14	15	16	17
18	19	20	21	22	23	24
25	26	27	28	29	30	21
1	2	3	4	5	6	7

WEEKLY ASSIGNMENTS 2016

Enter class, title and information for specific assignments/projects that are due this week.

MON 4
_____
_____
_____

WEEKLY SCHEDULE

	MON	TUES	WED	THURS	FRI
8:00AM					
9:00AM					
10:00AM					
11:00AM		11:00AM ACA 122		11:00AM ACA 122	
12 NOON					
1:00PM					
2:00PM					
3:00PM					
4:00PM					
5:00PM					
6:00PM					

TUES 19 ACA 122 Weekly Calendar and Task List
- must be submitted in BB before class begins on _____
Ex. 1.3 in course textbooks.

WED
_____
_____
_____

THU
_____
_____
_____

FRI
_____
_____
_____

Now it's time to look at whether you are or are not allocating enough time to those things most important to you. If you were to take another look at your last seven days, how important would this reflection say your education is to you? With the many tasks, events and obligations contending for your time and energy every day, you must prioritize.

Make a list of your daily or weekly tasks and prioritize according to the descriptions below.
Extremely Important=3   Important=2   Slightly Important=1

1. Brainstorm tasks. Make a list of all the tasks to get done.
2. Estimate time. Determine how long each task will take and be realistic about it.
3. Rate each task by priority: 3 Extremely important, 2 Important, 1 Slightly important.
4. Cross off tasks as you complete them. Keep the list with you.
5. Evaluate at the end of each day.

DAILY TASKS	APPROX. TIME	PRIORITY

STEP 4 — Track Your Progress

Based on what you have learned in this section about time management and about yourself, take a moment to think about how you can use this information to improve your time effectiveness. When answering the questions below, consider specific things that you do well and explain precisely what you need to do to improve.

1. Where did you waste time?

2. Which time tracking tool or calendar do you prefer?

3. What should you **STOP** doing?

4. What should you **KEEP** doing?

5. What should you **START** doing?

CRITICAL THINKING and DECISION MAKING

Critical thinking is our ability to utilize thinking that is clear, rational, open-minded and informed by evidence. It incorporates the active, skillful deployment of the general principles and procedures of thinking which are most conducive to obtaining truth and accuracy in judgment. Simply put: Critical thinking is thorough thinking. A critical thinker is able to get past biases and view situations from different perspectives to ultimately improve one's understanding of the world.

The foundation of critical thinking is understanding how evidence supports or opposes a claim/position/decision. In essence, how information is relevant to whether a claim is true or false.

A Critical Thinker:

➜ Asks appropriate questions such as: What am I being asked to accept? Should I accept it or not? Why? What are the arguments and how strong are they?

➜ Gathers relevant information

➜ Efficiently and creatively sorts through the information

➜ Reasons logically based on the information

➜ Comes to reliable and trustworthy conclusions

An UNcritical Thinker:

➜ Accepts things purely on faith

➜ Thinks a person's beliefs are "true for them" and can't be mistaken or criticized

➜ Is not disposed to seek evidence or challenge beliefs

CHARACTERISTICS OF AN EFFECTIVE CRITICAL THINKER

- Uses evidence skillfully and impartially

- Organizes thoughts and articulates them concisely and coherently

- Distinguishes between logically valid and invalid inferences

- Suspends judgment in the absence of sufficient evidence to support a decision

- Understands the difference between reasoning and rationalizing

- Possesses self-conviction

- Utilizes effective problem-solving skills

CRITICAL THINKING SKILLS

Analytical Thinking: The ability to analyze and examine information. Also incorporates thinking actively. How can we more effectively deal with life's situations?

Active Listening: The ability to make a conscious effort to understand/confirm what one is saying. Shows genuine interest when others are speaking. Uses clarifying questions, nods head, etc.

Investigative Ability: The ability to examine and explore situations. To ask why. What does the evidence say? What questions do I need to ask and answer to arrive at a conclusion?

Self Confidence and Conviction: The ability to think for ourselves and the conviction of our principles. What are my conclusions? Does this compromise my morals and beliefs?

Open Minded/Objective: The ability to openly view situations from different perspectives. Reflects an awareness of the ideas, views and opinions of others during discussions. What do the others think?

Effective Communication: The ability to articulate one's insight, opinions and ideas during discussions.

The Critical Thinking Map **AT WORK**

Here is an example of how critical thinking works, using an example of a student trying to decide which university is best for his or her transfer needs.

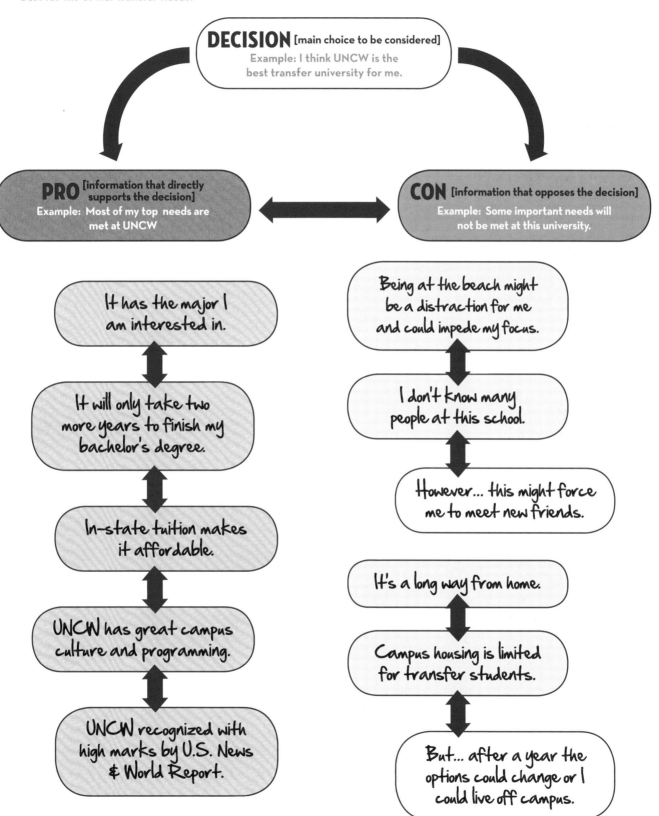

DECISION [main choice to be considered]
Example: I think UNCW is the best transfer university for me.

PRO [information that directly supports the decision]
Example: Most of my top needs are met at UNCW

CON [information that opposes the decision]
Example: Some important needs will not be met at this university.

It has the major I am interested in.

It will only take two more years to finish my bachelor's degree.

In-state tuition makes it affordable.

UNCW has great campus culture and programming.

UNCW recognized with high marks by U.S. News & World Report.

Being at the beach might be a distraction for me and could impede my focus.

I don't know many people at this school.

However... this might force me to meet new friends.

It's a long way from home.

Campus housing is limited for transfer students.

But... after a year the options could change or I could live off campus.

Making **DECISIONS**

Critical thinking leads to effective decision making. Throughout your college experience and life, you will be confronted with the inevitable need to make decisions. This can be an overwhelming task that if not done properly, can have unfavorable results.

As you work through the decisions mentioned before, it is helpful if you know your decision-making style and process. How have you made decisions in the past? Are you analytical or do you go with your "gut?" Do you overanalyze and get into analysis paralysis? Do you like to talk things over with many people in your life or sit and think quietly on your own?

DECISION MAKING STYLES

Planning, weighing the facts, logical thinking

Trusting your gut or intuition

Defaulting, playing it safe

Pleasing others, compliant, letting others decide

Avoidance or procrastination, delaying

Impulsive, don't look before you leap!

Agonizing, what if, analysis paralysis!

Think about three decisions you have made in the last week. Provide a short response for the following questions.

Which of these styles did you use?

Which of these styles do you use most often?

THE DECISION MAKING PROCESS

There is a formal process to help you make effective decisions. The **Decision Making Process** is the cognitive process of choosing between alternative courses of action. Now let's take a look at the steps to effective decision making!

STEP 1 Define and State the Real Issue

This is your opportunity to define and clarify the real issue. To do this properly, you must first determine if you are dealing with the important or relevant aspects of an issue or if you are just focusing on the visible symptoms. Problems are often the symptom and not the true problem. For example, not getting the internship of your choice (symptom) may reflect not submitting a strong application (problem); your rejection for admission to your number one college choice (symptom) may be because you waited until the last minute to work on your applications or because you did not prepare for the SAT (problem).

Take time to think about what your issue is. This is not a time for haste, but for careful inspection and deliberation. Start to determine conditions of the ideal solution and balance long-range goals. You might even find it necessary to change traditional approaches.

STEP 2   Investigate and Analyze the Issue

In this step you will identify specific elements contributing to the issue/problem that must be found and changed. Be sure you gather all the facts and understand what they mean.

Establish goals that solving the problem should accomplish and determine the requirements that the solution to the problem must meet. Ask yourself: what are the goals that resolving this issue should accomplish? This is also an opportunity to investigate and eliminate undesirable or unwise courses of action.

STEP 3   Develop Possible Solutions

To begin this step, brainstorm possible options and solutions. Develop several alternative solutions for the issue and avoid "either-or" plans. This forces us to test the validity of our basic assumptions. It does not necessarily guarantee a right decision, but at least the problem has been thought through.

Remember that sometimes, to take no action at all may be one of the alternatives. This requires a decision too. However, it should not be done just to avoid something unpleasant.

STEP 4   Determine the Best Solution

It is rare for an issue to have only one solution. The challenge is to select the best solution for you. Always make the best decision in light of the given facts. Consider using the technique of comparing the pros and cons of each option. To do this use the Critical Thinking Map on page 19 as a reference. This will help you think through and determine which solution seems to offer the best results with the least disturbance to your goals. Weigh your pros and cons by identifying the options or possible solutions. Then list the pros and cons for each of the possible solutions.

Remember, even the best solution has its risks and gains. Appraise the odds of each alternative. Also, be prepared to correct the decision if new information indicates a change in status. Some questions you might ask yourself during this step are:
→   What is the potential impact this decision will have?
→   Will this solution serve long-term needs?

STEP 5   Translate the Decision into Effective Action

Here is where you create a plan for your decision and realize it. Consider time a factor. You should be cognizant of deadlines and be sure it can be accomplished in a realistic period of time. Be prepared to explain your decision to those involved and affected. And always follow up to ensure proper and effective implementation as well as evaluating the effects of the decision you made.

EXERCISE 1.1B | MY **CRITICAL THINKING** MAP

Choose any decision that you need to make related to your university transfer. Examples might include: Should I live on or off campus? Which university is best for me? Should I take out a student loan? Which fraternity/sorority is best for me?

Use the Critical Thinking Map (page 19) as a reference to create your own Critical Thinking Map in the space provided below. Weigh the pros and cons to help determine the best solution.

The Student CODE OF CONDUCT and ACADEMIC INTEGRITY

Part of taking responsibility as a student is being honest and exhibiting behaviors that reflect positively on yourself and your institution. Having academic integrity and knowing the student code of conduct will help you in this endeavor. Colleges reserve the right to maintain a safe and orderly learning environment for students, faculty and staff. Therefore, students are expected to conduct themselves in a manner reflecting a civilized society.

The Student Code of Conduct describes student rights and responsibilities, procedures, prohibited behaviors and sanctions that can be used when a student is found responsible for violations. Some of the policies you will read about in the code of conduct include academic dishonesty, student behavior, drugs, alcohol and tobacco policies, and use of college property.

Make sure you know how to access the student handbook/code of conduct for your college. You should always know where to find the college policies that apply to your status as a student on whatever college campus you decide to attend. You need to be familiar with the academic integrity policy, the code of conduct and honor codes that may be a part of your campus culture as well as where you can get help if needed. These documents also discuss your rights as a student, including how to appeal grades or other academic or disciplinary actions.

Some examples of prohibited behaviors on college campuses include:
➔ Violence, harassment, disruption, failure to comply
➔ Sexual misconduct
➔ Possession or use of illegal drugs or alcohol
➔ Violation of weapons policy

Possible sanctions for code of conduct violations might include:
➔ Probation
➔ Suspension
➔ Expulsion

ACADEMIC INTEGRITY:

What is academic integrity? It is the ethical code or policy of academic scholarship. This policy incorporates values such as the avoidance of cheating or plagiarism, maintenance of satisfactory academic standards, and honesty and rigor in academic research and publishing.

Your college expects absolute integrity and personal honor in all students' academic work! Here are some of the specific behaviors you want to avoid:

Cheating: The intentional use or attempt to use unauthorized materials, information, notes, study aids or other devices in any academic exercise and includes the unauthorized communication of information during an academic exercise.

Plagiarism: The practice of taking someone else's work or ideas and passing them off as one's own. There are four types of plagiarism:

> **1. Unintentional:** writer intends to cite but doesn't know how to do so properly.

> **2. Cyber-downloading:** work from a website without giving credit to author.

> **3. Intentional:** writer deliberately copies work and takes credit for it.

> **4. Self:** writer copies his/her own work and presents it as something new.

Complicity in academic dishonesty: intentionally or knowingly helping or attempting to help another to commit an act of academic dishonesty.

Fabrication and falsification: the intentional and unauthorized invention of alteration of any information or citation in an academic exercise. Fabrication is a matter of inventing or counterfeiting information for use in any academic exercise; falsification is a matter of altering information.

AVOID PLAGIARISM

- Be careful when citing electronic sources.

- Don't assume the information you find on the Internet is common knowledge.

- When evaluating electronic sources always ask if the information is reliable.

- Wikipedia and other wikis are collaborative information sites contributed to by a variety of people. They are not considered reliable sources for academic citation and should not be used as sources in an academic paper.

Abuse of academic materials: making inaccessible, destroying or stealing library or other academic resource material, including equipment. Violations may be referred to civil authorities for prosecution under the law.

Installation of a computer virus: rendering ineffective or inaccessible or destroying computer software and/or databases through the installation of a computer virus.

There are consequences of not adhering to the Academic Integrity Policy. This is often called **Academic Misconduct**. Some possible consequences include:

➔ Redoing or failing an assignment.

➔ Reduction to final grade in course.

➔ Failing the course with a grade of "F."

➔ Recommendation to a remediation program.

➔ Loss of scholarships.

➔ Being dismissed from the class or the college.

➔ Having a record of academic dishonesty/misconduct on transcript.

Adapted from CPCC Academic Integrity Policy, www.cpcc.edu

SEXUAL ASSAULT, STALKING AND DOMESTIC VIOLENCE:

As a recipient of federal funds, all colleges and universities are required to comply with Title IX of the Higher Education Amendments of 1972, 20 U.S.C. § 1681 et seq. ("Title IX"), which prohibits discrimination on the basis of sex in educational programs or activities, admissions and employment.

Unlawful discriminatory behaviors under Title IX include, but are not limited to:

1. Sexual Harassment (unwelcome sexual advances, requests for sexual favors and other verbal or physical conduct of a sexual nature);

2. Sexual Misconduct (rape, sexual assault, sexual battery, sexual exploitation and other forms of non-consensual sexual activity);

3. Stalking (repeatedly following, harassing, threatening or intimidating, including by telephone, email, electronic communication, or social media);

4. Dating Violence (including emotional, verbal and economic abuse without the presence of physical abuse); and

5. Retaliation (adverse employment, academic or other actions against anyone reporting or participating in an investigation of Title IX allegations).

The following are examples of types of conduct that may constitute sexual harassment:

1. Inappropriate touching, patting or pinching

2. Physical assault or coerced sexual activity

3. Demands or subtle pressure for sexual favors

4. Unwanted phone calls, texts, email or gestures

If you feel you are the victim of any type of sexual harassment or misconduct, please contact an instructor, a college counselor, the Office of Student Conduct and Civility, the Title IX coordinator or campus security at your school. *Adapted from CPCC Title IX Policies and Procedures, www.cpcc.edu*

SATISFACTORY ACADEMIC STANDING

Students are expected to achieve certain minimum levels of progress toward the successful academic completion of course requirements for a degree, certificate or diploma to graduate. In addition, federal regulations require institutions to establish minimum standards of satisfactory progress for students receiving financial aid. For example at many colleges, potential graduates must have earned a minimum overall grade point average (GPA) of 2.0 out of a possible 4.0 to be eligible for graduation.

Each college has a series of levels that constitute your academic standing. Make sure to check your college for their specific policies about what it means to be in "good standing." Also note what happens if you fall below the GPA required to be in good standing and how this can affect your financial aid. Here are some common classifications of academic standing that are used at many colleges:

→ Good Standing
→ Academic Warning
→ Academic Probation
→ Academic Suspension

CALCULATING YOUR GPA (GRADE POINT AVERAGE)

You may have several types of GPAs that appear on your student record: the cumulative GPA, program GPA and term GPA. All are calculated using the same formula.

Each course grade is worth a certain number of quality points. Quality points for a given course are determined by multiplying the credit hours earned in the course by the grade point value shown below:

A = 4 points
B = 3 points
C = 2 points
D = 1 point
F = 0 points

The Formula

An "A" grade earned in a three-credit course would be worth 12 quality points:

3 credits x 4 (Grade A) = 12 quality points

To determine your GPA:

→ Add the total quality points for all of the courses.

→ Divide the total number of quality points by the total number of credits for the courses.

EXAMPLE OF GRADE POINT AVERAGE CALCULATION				
SUBJECT	**HOURS OR CREDITS**	**GRADE RECEIVED**	**POINTS PER GRADE**	**QUALITY POINTS**
English	3	A	4	12
Communications	3	B	3	9
Economics	3	B	3	9
Biology	4	D	1	4
Psychology	3	C	2	6
TOTAL	**16**			**40**

GPA is 40 / 16 = 2.5

EXERCISE 1.1C | ACADEMIC **STATUS** AND **GPA**

In this exercise you will investigate your current academic status and learn how to calculate your GPA.

1. What is the minimum GPA requirement at your college in order to maintain satisfactory status?

2. Go to your personal account at your college and find your academic status information. This information may be located under Standards of Academic Progress.

    a. What is your current academic status?

    b. Are you eligible to register for classes next semester?

3. What is your cumulative GPA?

4. What is your goal GPA for the current semester?

Project Your Semester GPA

In the grid below, list each of the classes in which you are currently enrolled and the number of credit hours for each class. Next you will predict the letter grade you must earn in each class, the point value for each grade and the total number of quality points for each class. Be sure to enter your totals.

COURSE & NUMBER	CREDIT HOURS	PROJECTED FINAL GRADE	POINT VALUE FOR GRADE	NUMBER OF QUALITY POINTS
TOTAL CREDIT HOURS:			TOTAL QUALITY POINTS:	

What is your projected semester GPA? (Be sure to show your work.)

PROJECTED GPA:	

"*Start where you are.*
Use what you have.   Do what you can."
—*arthur ashe*

SECTION 2 | NAVIGATING COLLEGE SYSTEMS & SUPPORT

IN THIS SECTION:

→ Identify College Tools and Systems

→ Discern How to Be Successful in Online Learning

→ Discover Student Support and Resources

→ Get Involved in Student Leadership and Civic Engagement

SECTION 2 | NAVIGATING COLLEGE SYSTEMS & SUPPORT

One of the things that will help you be successful at college is understanding and being able to navigate the systems and tools used for student learning and support. Below are examples of these tools and suggestions on how to use them OR where to go to get additional assistance. One number you want to have on speed dial in your phone is the college's "Help Desk" for computer and technical questions and issues. They can also help you if you are having problems logging into your college accounts and systems.

1. Setting up your college account

To get started, you need to set up your college account. First, you will need a username (usually assigned by the college) and password (created by you). After creating your account, you will have access to the college's main access point for items such as online registration, financial aid resources, looking up your Grade Point Average (GPA), transcripts, and your class schedule or program of study. Each college has a unique name for this access. Some examples are: My College at Central Piedmont Community College, myWAKETECH at WakeTech Community College or MyRCC Login at Robeson Community College.

2. Being able to access and use the College Catalog

Every college has a catalog that is the "one-stop shop" for everything about the college. Here you can learn about the history of the college, the programs of study, all the courses offered at the college as well as support resources for learning, student life and career assistance. Let's take a look at two important pieces of the catalog.

Course Description

Every course will have a description that tells you the summary of what the course covers and also any prerequisites for the course. A prerequisite is a course that must be taken before another one. It is important to know these requirements as you may not be able to register for a class if you have not met the prerequisites. Also, courses are abbreviated with three letters (English is ENG, History is HIS). This is followed by a number: English 111 or History 132. Remember you can go to the College Catalog at any point and read the description to ensure you are signing up for the right course.

Programs of Study

A Program of Study is the curriculum, or list of courses, you need to take to acquire a particular degree, diploma or certificate. You choose the program based on your career and educational goals. Two of the key transfer programs at the community college level are the Associate of Arts and and Associate of Science degrees.

3. Understanding the registration process

Registering for your classes is an important step in getting started at college. After meeting with an academic advisor about what classes to take, you will need to find out how to register. Can you register online? What are the timelines? Is there priority registration timing given for students who have been in school longer? Make sure to ask about the timeline for paying for your classes. Is the payment for classes due at registration or do you have a few weeks to make payment? You do not want to have your classes "dropped" due to non-payment.

Another term you will hear about when discussing courses is the "section" number. All courses have a number and section attached. For example, you may be taking English 111 which is "Writing and Inquiry." Colleges use the numbers to help differentiate between courses. When you are registering you will also see there are many options for taking English 111 depending on the time, day, etc. These are called sections. There may be 80 sections of a course and you need to pick the one that fits best into your schedule. So the actual class may say ENG 111-10. That is English 111 section 10.

It is also important that you know the college policies related to the drop/add period and class withdrawals that apply to your status as a student. The drop/add period is usually the first couple of days in the beginning of the semester when you can drop a current class in which you are enrolled. A withdrawal is when you have a limited time to formally withdraw from your class or classes. Remember, it's the student's responsibility to initiate procedures leading to a formal withdrawal ("W") in order to avoid a failing ("F") grade. There are always dates that apply and must be honored.

4. Knowing how to use the Learning Management System (LMS)

Every college uses a learning management system, also known as the LMS. Some examples of this system are Blackboard and Moodle. This online system provides you with access to your courses and learning material, provides a way for you to communicate with classmates and allows you to submit assignments and view your grades. Even if you are taking a traditional face-to-face class, most use a learning management system so you will need to become familiar with how to access and use this technology. Here are some basic tips for working in your college's learning management system.

→ Take advantage of any orientation or training on how to use the system.

→ Make sure you know your username and password and that you can log in to your learning management system.

→ Take time to review the course homepage. Notice what is personalized for you. See what types of activities, announcements, course-related content and other information are available on the main page. Also be sure to check for any messages the school administrators or your instructors may have sent.

→ All your classes should also be listed for you; if not, verify when that information will be available. Choose one course to explore. Observe the features in the navigation bars, and see what information appears as you navigate through those items.

→ Take a closer look at how the course materials are presented. Note if you have any material to review, read, or watch for the weekly assignments; learn how you'll take in the lecture material; make note of the frequency and due dates for tests, assignments and other activities; and find out how class discussion will take place. Learn how the course is structured (Weeks? Units?) and determine whether you can work ahead or not. Learn about the grading and point system for all the assignments.

→ Discover how you'll communicate with your instructor and fellow students. Become familiar with all forms of messaging, including chat, asynchronous discussion or discussion boards and email. Also, be sure you know and understand how discussion boards are graded.

5. Learning to read a Syllabus

You may be familiar with how to read a syllabus but if you are not, this is one skill you want to learn quickly. A syllabus is the official document that outlines the requirements and policies of each of your courses. You should receive a copy of the syllabus on the first day of class from your instructor. It is considered the "contract" about how the class operates, what the instructor's expectations are for the students in the class and your responsibilities as a student.

Some of the important items you might find in the syllabus are: dates and times for the course, instructor contact information, course description, objectives and outline of the course; information about the textbook or other resources being used, attendance requirements, information and expectations about assignments and deadlines, and policies for the class or college. If there are any disagreements or appeals related to any class policies or grade, the syllabus is used to assist in making the final decision.

How to be Successful in **ONLINE LEARNING**

In college you will likely have the option of taking classes in person or online. Online learning can provide you with many advantages. Do you need to take classes at night or on the weekends? Do you need flexibility due to work or family commitments? Is it difficult for you to get to campus to attend classes? Do you want the freedom to complete your classes at the time and place of your choosing? If you answered "yes" to any of these questions, online learning may work well with your lifestyle.

However, it is also crucial you think about not only what you need, but also what you are willing and able to do. Online learning is not just going to class in your pajamas! It requires a skills set that includes being an independent, self-directed learner who is comfortable with technology and has effective time management skills. Let's take a look at some of the basic requirements for online learners.

"Students can *often misunderstand the online learning environment* and lack the requisite study and student success skills they need to succeed," the report said. "They can be tech-savvy when using social media and communications tools, but lack the necessary basic computer skills to take online courses."
— "GOING THE DISTANCE" BY PAUL BRADLEY
EDITOR, COMMUNITY COLLEGE WEEK , MAY 27, 2015

TECHNOLOGY

As a student enrolled in an online course you are expected to have access to basic technologies and possess basic computer skills. These include:

→ Regular and reliable access to a computer (PC or laptop) and the Internet. If you do not have access in your home, check at your school for student labs or library computer resources; your local library may serve this purpose. Please note they often have time restrictions and limited hours, so plan accordingly.

→ Document writing software, preferably Microsoft Word. Check with your college to see if you can receive student discounts on software products.

→ The ability to navigate the Internet (locating a website), basic word processing and file exchange (uploading and downloading) via Blackboard, Moodle or an other learning management system site. Check with your college for tutorials, orientations or other resources they provide for students to become proficient in an online learning environment.

→ The ability to download and access more than one browser. Blackboard performs best when using Firefox as your browser. While Internet Explorer, Google Chrome and Safari can be used, students have experienced glitches and problems with Blackboard in these browsers. If you experience technical problems while in Blackboard, please contact the Information Technology Services Helpdesk at your school for assistance or try using a different browser.

→ Make sure to use your college email account to communicate with your instructors. It is important to use your student email account to send and receive messages in your courses.

→ Check your email account often, especially if you have been put on a wait list to enroll in courses. Your college may notify you of an open spot using email, and you must respond within a certain amount of time.

→ Do not rely on using your smartphone to access and participate in your course. Some colleges do not allow mobile device connections and some assignments may be challenging to complete with accuracy using your phone.

TIME MANAGEMENT and PERSONAL RESPONSIBILITY

Earlier in Section 1 of this unit, you learned about the importance of personal responsibility. Below you will find additional tips for taking personal responsibility as it relates specifically to your success in online learning.

→ Depending on your course, you may be required to take a quiz or complete an assignment within the first week of class before you can view your course material and assignments. This is the college's way of knowing that you've "shown up" for class. Check each course as soon as you log in to see if your course requires this. If you don't take the quiz within the allotted time, you might be dropped from the class.

→ Ask yourself if you possess the following characteristics of successful online students: independent, self-disciplined, persistent, able to manage your own time and due dates, etc.

→ Talk with those you live with to ask for support and time to do your online assignments.

→ Schedule time to complete your work. Sometimes it is easy to "forget" you have an online class so make sure to plan this into your weekly schedule.

→ Ask for help from your instructor or your technology support resources if you have any questions.

→ Ensure you use proper netiquette when completing any writing assignments or discussion boards in your online classes. For more information about netiquette, visit **http://www.carnegiecyberacademy.com** and search for netiquette. Take Betty's Netiquette Quiz for a fun way to get familiar with netiquette guidelines.

EXERCISE 1.2A | **ARE YOU READY** FOR ONLINE LEARNING?

Are you ready to be an online student? Choose the answer next to each answer that best describes you.

My personal schedule is:

1. Pretty easy to predict. I know when I have 2-3 hours at a time to devote to my coursework.

2. Usually predictable. Occasionally, something will come up at the last minute, but I can shift other things around in my schedule so I can get chunks of time for myself.

3. Typically up in the air. Because of my responsibilities as a parent and/or frequent and sudden changes in work schedule, finding 2-3 hours to myself is challenging.

In a typical week, I can find _____ time to devote to studying and classwork.

1. At least 15 hours

2. 10-15 hours

3. Less than 10 hours

When it comes to managing my time as a student:

1. I know how to minimize distractions so I can stay focused. Sometimes, I even turn in my assignments ahead of time. My teachers typically don't have to remind me to finish my assignments.

2. I consider this to be an area I can improve upon. Sometimes I need help staying focused, but I typically get my work done right on time.

3. Yikes! I really need help staying focused. Time just seems to fly by without being able to complete much of my work.

My reading and writing skills are:

1. Excellent. After I read an article, I typically understand it and can easily and clearly explain key points to someone else either verbally or in written form.

2. Middle of the road. After I read an article, I sometimes need help understanding key points and explaining it to someone else either verbally or in written form

3. I need a lot of help in this area. After reading an article, I typically need help understanding key points and explaining it to someone else either verbally or in written form.

If I don't understand something explained in class:

1. I feel comfortable asking the instructor what he/she meant. I'm okay sending an email or picking up the phone to ask for more information or clarification.

2. I feel somewhat comfortable asking the instructor questions. I don't want to sound silly or unintelligent, but if I need help, I'll send an email or call them.

3. I have a hard time admitting to the instructor that I don't understand the material and seldom reach out for help.

I would describe my relationship with computers as:

1. Best friends status. I use the computer regularly and have no problem using multiple tabs within browsers, sending email with attachments and using word processors (ex. Word). If my instructor were to put my course materials inside an online site I have to log in to, I could probably figure out how to use the site by watching online videos, asking a few questions or clicking around.

2. Courteous and on good terms. I use the computer for the things I need (sending an email to my friends, creating documents for an organization that I volunteer with). I can use the Internet, but go to specific websites and don't do much exploring. If my instructor were to put my course materials inside an online site I have to log in to, I would probably look for training or specific directions before clicking around.

3. Rocky. I don't use the computer much, so if my instructor were to put my course materials inside an online site I have to log in to, I would probably get overwhelmed easily. I would probably want someone to sit down with me and provide one-on-one help as I complete my assignments.

My access to the Internet is:
1. Readily available: I have high-speed Internet at home. If that goes out, I have no problem going to the local library to use their computers or Wi-Fi connections. I have a computer, laptop or Mac and know how to get access to a second computer if mine crashes.

2. Somewhat available: I have high-speed Internet at home, but I'll need to identify how I can get access if it goes out. I also have access to a computer, laptop, or Mac, but need to figure out how to access a second one if my personal computer crashes.

3. Occasionally available: I don't have high-speed Internet at home, and often have to rely on using Wi-Fi or the Internet at local restaurants or libraries. I don't have a computer, laptop or Mac and don't know how I can get access to one.

Now, count the number of 1s, 2s, and 3s in your answers and record them here:

_____3_____ 1   _____4_____ 2   _____0_____ 3

If you answered mostly 1s: You already have the habits and resourcefulness necessary to be a successful online student. A good online student has discipline, plans his or her time wisely and allows extra time to turn in assignments in case technology fails. It's great you can easily identify chunks of time to devote to group and solo work. Also, being willing to ask questions and dialogue with people you may never meet in-person is important in an online class.

If you answered mostly 2s: You have some of the habits of a good online student and can learn some of the other habits and skills necessary to participate in an online class. Review all of the #1 statements. These actions will need to make their way into your study habits if your goal is to fully learn the material and pass your course. You might consider taking a hybrid course so you get the traditional face-to-face classroom instruction and necessary online experience before making the leap fully online. Also, be sure to communicate your needs with an academic advisor or success coach at your school throughout the semester to make sure you stay on track and focused.

If you answered mostly 3s: Some of your answers suggest you would be more successful in a traditional classroom that allows you to interact face to face. Some traditional classroom instructors post material online, which makes it possible for you to gradually learn skills and develop habits that will make you a successful online student. Review all of the #1 statements. Whether you're taking a course online or in a traditional classroom, these actions will need to make their way into your study habits in order to be successful.

Now that you have your score, take a minute to dive deeper by checking off the skills below you are already proficient in. For any you cannot answer "yes" to, make sure you find the resources you need to build your skills so you can become a successful online learner.

Computer and Technology Skills

_____ I have access to a computer with a reliable Internet connection.

_____ I know how to start up and shut down a computer.

_____ I know how to identify and use icons, windows and menus on my computer desktop.

_____ I am capable of sending and receiving email.

_____ I know how to attach files to an email message.

_____ I understand how to navigate the Internet and use Web browsers.

_____ I am capable of using standard word processing software, including entering, copying and pasting text.

_____ I am capable of opening, saving, copying and storing documents and can retrieve them as needed.

_____ I can install and uninstall software when necessary.

_____ I know how to access the Technical Support Help Desk for my college.

_____ I know how to access and navigate the learning management system for my college (such as Blackboard or Moodle).

_____ I am capable of submitting an assignment in our learning management system (Blackboard or Moodle).

_____ I know how to use online discussions and forums.

Personal Readiness

_____ I am an effective time manager and have a process for keeping track of my assignments.

_____ I am capable of prioritizing my responsibilities.

_____ I am goal-oriented and have persistence to reach my goals even when faced with obstacles.

_____ I am self-motivated and disciplined when it comes to my studies.

_____ I take responsibility and am committed to my learning and education.

_____ I can learn by working independently.

_____ I am willing and able to express my opinion in writing.

_____ I am not afraid to ask for help from the instructor or other support areas if needed.

_____ I am comfortable learning material by reading or watching videos.

_____ I am capable of and willing to learn new technologies.

Online Learning Readiness Exercise developed in conjunction with Joy Scott, Instructional Developer in eLearning, Central Piedmont Community College

STUDENT SUPPORT and RESOURCES

Student Affairs

Robert D. Brown, 50th president of the American College Personnel Association, said cognitive and personal development on the collegiate level has been viewed as highly interlaced and the whole student has been considered more than the educated parts. Student Affairs focuses on developing the whole student. It is the goal of promoting a marriage between the growth of intellectual development in the classroom and social development outside the classroom. Student Affairs is a department or division of support services available to students at institutions of higher education. The programs and services are designed to enhance student growth and development for student success and degree completion. Student Affairs should work in collaboration with academic programs to provide opportunities for students to explore student life, health and wellness, leadership and service, civic engagement, and diversity.

The beginning of Student Affairs has been traced back to Athenian education and universities in The Middle Ages. In early American colleges, "in loco parentis," which means "in place of the parent," was the approach used to support students by acting as the parent while the student was attending college away from home. Through this approach, the focus was on control of the student, as opposed to the modern philosophy which focuses on the development of the student as a whole. (Delworth, Hanson and Associates, 1989)

→ Enhance student growth and development

→ Promote student success and degree completion

→ Ensure a richer college experience

→ Help students develop skills outside the classroom

Depending on the college culture and climate, departments for Student Affairs will vary in service areas. Some of the more common areas include:

Academic Advising

Helps students translate academic requirements established in the College Catalog into an academic plan specific to program and major. Well qualified advisors will assist you with navigating your academic and degree requirements. Ultimately, the onus is on the student to make decisions about his/her academic and career goals.

Academic Learning Center/Tutoring

Enhances the students' chances of academic success by helping them reach their full academic potential. It's designed to help students discover how to learn and function more effectively as college students. These centers offer services for those with learning challenges in a particular discipline or who simply wish to increase their learning skills. Services include, but may not be limited to, tutoring, specialized academic labs and study/learning strategies, test-taking tips and services.

Counseling Services

Provides emotional and psychological support to students facing challenges through short-term counseling and provides referrals when more in-depth therapy is required. Credentialed and well-trained counselors are there to provide a safe environment for students to freely discuss and explore in complete confidence, any problems, feelings or fears. The ultimate goal is to help students develop self-understanding that will aid in their ability to better cope with immediate and future decisions.

Disability Services

Works with all areas of the college to ensure students with disabilities can succeed independently in meeting the demands of college life. They provide access and accommodations for students with documented disabilities that allows equal opportunity for participation in all college classes, programs, activities, events, services, campus facilities, curriculum and technology. Disability Services has qualified professionals available to help identify and address physical, communication, learning and information barriers. In addition, they promote an inclusive campus community, make referrals and provide advocacy support as needed.

Library Services

Serves as an integral part of your educational learning experience by providing information, resources and services. It houses outstanding collections of books, periodicals, research databases, audio-visual and electronic materials, college archives and special collections that support the programs and courses offered at your community college. In order to develop information literacy, most also offer instruction in the use of libraries and research techniques. Physical space is provided for individual and group study sessions. Faculty and students' needs are met by qualified professionals and support staff regardless of class location and delivery style.

Registration

Also known as the Office of the Registrar. It supports teaching and learning by maintaining the integrity of academic policies. This is the area responsible for processing registration requests, scheduling classes and maintaining course offerings, enforcing the rules for enrolling or withdrawing classes, and keeping a permanent record of grades and college transcripts.

Some other areas that exist under the Student Affairs umbrella are:

- → **Campus Ministries** provides spiritual guidance and comfort to students in need.
- → **Campus Police/Security** provides a safe campus environment for college students, faculty and staff.
- → **Greek Life** (Fraternities and Sororities) is responsible for managing and advising the entire Greek community at the university.
- → **Health and Wellness** promotes and advocates for students' physical, emotional and psychological health and awareness.
- → **Housing/Residence Life** provides on-campus housing for students with programming that promotes personal, social, educational and cultural development.
- → **Intramural Sports** is responsible for club team sports usually sponsored by the Campus Intramural or Recreation department. Men's, women's and co-ed (men and women) teams of all different skill levels compete in a variety of sports.
- → **International Student Services** assists F-1 international students in setting up life in the U.S. and assists in their adjustment to college life.
- → **Multicultural Affairs** promotes diversity and inclusion among college students, faculty and staff.
- → **Student Activities and Programming** provides campus-wide programs and events that promote educational, cultural and social development.

STUDENT LEADERSHIP and CIVIC ENGAGEMENT

One of the most important aspects of student development is that which happens outside the classroom. Student leadership and civic engagement are arguably the most beneficial extracurricular activities a student can perform while in college. Student leadership is a learning environment that encourages hands-on experiential learning and development. Organizing and planning, critical thinking and problem solving, effective communication, and working with and leading teams are some of the portable leadership skills students build while engaged in leadership and civic responsibilities. As a prospective transfer student, it is beneficial to note that colleges and universities look favorably upon students who demonstrate evidence of leadership and personal development during their college experience.

Here are some ways you can get involved in leadership opportunities at your college:

➔ Student Government Association (SGA)   ➔ Clubs and Organizations

➔ Learning Communities   ➔ Fraternities and Sororities

➔ Service Learning

The rich experience of student leadership and civic engagement will work well for you beyond college. The skills mentioned can easily be transferred into the professional arena once you complete your college experience. In fact, these are skills that companies find valuable in graduates they are considering for employment.

Students who have participated in leadership and civic opportunities often find:

➔ They are better prepared for the workforce

➔ They often become industry leaders

➔ They have more career marketability

For example, college students may worry because they do not always have the extensive work experience employers are looking for when they attempt to seek employment. There are many ways to get experience that will gain the attention of hiring managers and recruiters. These include internships, co-ops, civic engagement, volunteer work, leadership, study abroad or research with faculty. All of these are experiences that can build skills and competencies that will give you a competitive edge during the interview process.

Remember that much of your development as a person occurs outside the classroom. Take advantage of programs, opportunities and services offered at your college or in your community to develop your leadership and interpersonal skills. Doing so will not only be beneficial to your career but also to your success as an individual.

EXERCISE 1.2B | STUDENT **SUPPORT**

Take a look at each scenario and match the support services area that could assist you if you were in the following situations.

Residence life	Career services	New/transfer student orientation
Counseling services	Student life/activities	Campus security
Financial aid	Greek affairs	Academic advising
Academic learning center	Admissions	Campus ministries

1. "This summer I should probably look for a job in my field. I should start looking at job options, working on my résumé and brushing up on my interviewing skills." _____

2. "I really miss my friends back home. All of these people are so different from me and there is nothing to do around here." _____

3. "I got enough money from the scholarship to pay for my first year of college but what about next year... how will I pay?" _____

4. "My dad has been a member of a fraternity since he was in college. He's an active member today and they do great service work in the community. I've always wanted to join too."
_____

5. "My roommate stays up really late at night and it keeps me up. I have an 8 a.m. class four times a week. I tried talking to her about it and things were better for a couple of weeks. Now she's back to old habits." _____

6. "I am having a lot of trouble with this chemistry class. Everyone said this instructor is the best one but I can't follow the lectures and there are 200 people in the class." _____

7. "I just heard from a friend that I need to take one more Spanish class to graduate. I thought I only needed one semester of a foreign language." _____

8. "This campus is huge. I'm overwhelmed by so many buildings. I don't know where anything is and just want to go back to my old community college. I'm comfortable there."
_____

9. "I'm not dealing well with a loss I recently suffered. I'm not motivated to go to class or even get out of bed." _____

10. "My evening class ends after dark. The campus is well-lit but maybe I should have an escort to my car."
_____

11. "I'd like to transfer to the university as an Engineering major. I wonder what I need to do to make it happen." _____

12. "I would like to meet people who share my spiritual views." _____

NOTES

"Education is the most *powerful weapon* which you can use to change the world."
— nelson mandela

SECTION 3 | **LEARNING STRATEGIES FOR ACADEMIC SUCCESS**

IN THIS SECTION:

➔ Understand the Culture of College-Level Learning

➔ Explore Effective Ways to Process Information and the Importance of Learning Styles

➔ Identify Learning Strategies for Academic Success

SECTION 3 | LEARNING STRATEGIES FOR ACADEMIC SUCCESS

The Culture of ADULT LEARNING

One of the most important aspects of your academic success in college is that you have an understanding of how you learn or best comprehend information. There are three basic elements related to your academic success in college.

1) **Understanding the difference between high school and college-level learning**
You are now an adult learner. This means you learn differently from what you experienced as a child. Learning at this level should be directed by you…the individual.

2) **Ascertaining your most effective way to process information**
You need to identify and embrace your learning style. Your learning style refers to your personal preference for discerning, collecting, deducing and organizing information.

3) **Recognizing the importance of assessing your learning strategies and study habits**
It is critical to use this assessment process to build upon your strengths and improve your weaknesses early in your college career to ensure future success.

Adult LEARNING THEORY

The first thing you should know about the college classroom is the difference in the learning culture from what you experienced as a youth. In the early 1970s, Malcolm Knowles introduced the United States to the concept that adults and children learn differently.

Pedagogy refers to the assumptions and strategies for teaching children. It literally means the art and science of teaching children. The theories and strategies that apply to adult learners refer to **andragogy**, which means the art and science of helping adults learn. Based on the work of Malcolm Knowles and E.C. Lindeman, andragogy is the basis for all learning at the collegiate level.

Adult learners have the need to connect learning to current and prior real life experiences and a need to direct themselves. They also have an orientation to learning that needs to be life centered and they get motivated by learning that satisfies their personal needs and goals.

The application to classroom and online learning includes your professors creating learning experiences that maximize student autonomy and minimize instruction, as you will acquire new information and build upon existing knowledge more effectively when encouraged to explore learning on your own.

What this means to you as a college student in this new learning environment is that the responsibility is now yours. You direct your educational experience; not your parents, not your teachers, not your counselors. It is time for you to be your own advocate.

In High School (PEDAGOGY)

→ Applies to elementary and secondary education

→ The student's learning is teacher-directed

→ The teacher decides what course content is important to learn and how it should be learned

→ In order to be promoted, the learner only needs to know what the teacher deems relevant

→ Others structure and manage student's time and class schedule

→ Teachers constantly remind students of deadlines and responsibilities and determine and guide student's priorities

→ A bell rings to remind students that it is time to go to their next scheduled class

→ Parents are required to grant permission for extracurricular activities or field trips off campus

→ Grades are sent to student's parents

→ Student behavior is closely monitored and controlled and behavioral problems are reported to the parent

→ Parents have complete access to the student's behavior and education records as well as the disclosure of aforementioned information

In College (ANDRAGOGY)

→ Applies to adult learners

→ Learning is student-directed

→ It is assumed that the student will be responsible for exhibiting the appropriate behavior and maturation

→ Learners need to know what, how and why information is relevant to their life and career goals

→ Students' life experiences become a part of the learning experience

→ The students decide how to manage their time, determines their course of study/major and when they take their classes

→ Grades are sent to the student who must also grant access to parents

→ The institution must have written permission from the student in order to release any personal information, grades and/or behavioral issues

Note: FERPA (Family Educational Rights and Privacy Act of 1974) is federal legislation in the United States that protects the privacy of students' personally identifiable information. The act applies to all educational institutions that receive federal funds.

Processing INFORMATION

Information processing theory compares our minds to a computer. We receive information, then analyze and decide what to do with it (process it), store it in our memory and at some point retrieve what we need for our lives. The key is how do we encode and file the information in a way that we are able to retrieve it when necessary. It is essential to understanding new and specific content in the college classroom. Discovering how you process information promotes more efficient learning. Your memory plays a key role in learning and we will discuss how to improve your memory skills later in this section. Here are four simplified steps to the process:

STEP 1 — Information is sensed and registered.

We sense or perceive something in our environment and decide whether or not to attend to it. Is it important? Is it stimulating? Is it perceivable?

STEP 2 — Information is momentarily held in short-term or working memory.

Research indicates that we can hold approximately seven "chunks" of information at any one time in working memory. Information will likely be lost if it is not actively used and/or rehearsed.

STEP 3 — Information is encoded and put in long-term memory.

Occurs while information is in working/short-term memory, is often connected to existing knowledge and filed for later retrieval.

STEP 4 — Information is retrieved.

Depending on how well it was encoded, information is retrieved with the right environmental cues. Keep in mind, well-organized information is easier to retrieve later.

Adapted from East Tennessee State University at http://www.etsu.edu/fsi/learning/infoprocessing.aspx.

Ways to Improve PROCESSING INFORMATION

→ Monitor your thinking processes and notice how it feels to pay attention when you are thinking about something.

→ Learn to make decisions about what information being presented in class is relevant. Pay attention to what is important/relevant and ignore what is not important/irrelevant.

→ Get to know your professor/instructor. Introduce yourself, ask how you can be successful in the class and inquire about the professor's teaching style. Take the initiative to meet with your professor halfway through the class for a progress report. When experiencing a professor's difficult delivery method or a difficult subject, be willing to expand your ways of learning. Embrace learning methods more conducive to the subject matter.

→ Be an engaged learner and an active participant in classroom learning. Pre-read your chapter before class. Write down questions you have about the reading. Underline key concepts, important dates or numbers. Sit in the front of the class and volunteer for discussion. Bring your textbook and notebook to each class, along with pens, pencils and highlighter. Take notes, and draw maps or diagrams. Don't be afraid to ask questions during class and seek opportunities to confirm that you understand the material.

IDENTIFYING Your Learning Styles

There are many ways in which students receive, comprehend and retain information, such as by hearing, by sight or by what they physically experience/practice doing. It is important to your academic success that you are able to identify and understand your learning style. Research has shown that students can perform better on tests if they change study habits to fit their own personal learning styles.

The three most common learning styles are auditory, kinesthetic and visual.

DID YOU KNOW?

People remember only about:

→ 10% of what they READ
→ 20% of what they HEAR
→ 30% of what they SEE

Retention is increased to 50% if they HEAR AND SEE something, as when watching a movie or a demonstration.

People generally remember:

→ 50% of what's DISCUSSED in groups
→ 75% of what they PRACTICE by doing
→ 90% of what they TEACH to someone else

(Edgar Dale)

Auditory learners use the left side of the brain and process information best through what they hear. If you are an auditory learner you probably prefer listening over reading and writing; like to read to yourself out loud; prefer oral directions; prefer hearing the news on the radio or television, rather than reading the newspaper; would rather record a lecture than take notes on it; and are usually more vocal in class.

Learning Strategies for AUDITORY LEARNERS:

→ Use word association to remember facts and time lines.
→ Record lectures.
→ Talk through difficult concepts.
→ Teach or explain concepts and information to others.
→ Watch content on videos.
→ Repeat facts and information with eyes closed.
→ Participate in group and class discussions.
→ Use recorded materials to practice languages.
→ Verbally record class notes after writing them.

Best at tests that have: written responses to lectures they've heard and oral exams.

Challenged when tests are: reading passages and writing answers about them in a timed test.

Kinesthetic learners use the right side of the brain to processes information best. They prefer hands-on experiences and use the sense of touch. They need to do it to learn it. If you are a kinesthetic learner you are probably well coordinated, move around a lot or use objects that you can squeeze or play with when listening to a lecture or studying. You can usually assemble things without reading directions as well.

Learning Strategies for KINESTHETIC LEARNERS:

→ Study in short blocks, take frequent breaks and move around.

→ Take classes with labs.

→ Participate in demonstrations, projects and role playing.

→ Visit educational sites/museums.

→ Study with others.

→ Use memory games.

→ Use flash cards to memorize.

Best at tests that have: short definitions, fill-ins, multiple choice.

Challenged when tests are: long tests and have essays.

Visual Learners use the right side of the brain and tend to learn better by observing and seeing information. If you are a visual learner you are probably good at spelling, but may forget names; need time to think before understanding a lecture or concept; like colors and fashion; dream in color; like and understand colorful charts; and prefer a quiet location for studying.

Learning Strategies for VISUAL LEARNERS:

→ Map out events in history or draw scientific process.

→ Make outlines or use the Cornell method for taking notes.

→ Take a picture of or copy what the professor writes on the board.

→ Ask the professor to diagram.

→ Take notes and make lists.

→ Watch videos, PowerPoints and Prezi videos.

→ Color code words, timelines and research notes.

→ Outline, highlight (only 10%) and circle words in reading.

→ Use flashcards.

Best at tests that have: show a process, uses diagrams, maps, charts and essays

Challenged when tests are: listen and responding

No matter what the discipline/subject matter or the delivery method of your professor, you need to know how to convert the information you need to learn to the way you learn best. When learning new or difficult information, it is a natural tendency to use the learning style you prefer. However, it's also important to be flexible in the practice of using other learning styles as needed. For example, you might be an auditory learner, but when learning math it is just as important to visually see all steps in the math problem and/or practice working through it.

In addition to knowing your learning style and utilizing strategies that align with your style, here are some basic study tips that can apply to all students.

STUDY STRATEGIES for Student Success

→ **Identify the "best time" and environment for studying.** Everyone has high and low periods of attention and concentration. Are you a "morning person" or a "night person?" Get to know yourself and use your power times to study; use the down times for routines such as laundry and errands.

→ **Break down difficult/overwhelming tasks into smaller pieces then put them together for completion.** Always study the most difficult subjects first. Plan out your English essay in advance and work on it in "chunks" vs. writing it all in one night.

→ **Study in shorter time blocks with short breaks in between.** This keeps you from becoming exhausted and "wasting time." It is efficient because during your breaks, the brain is still processing the information.

→ **Make sure the environment is conducive to studying.** Choose a location that is isolated, spacious for spreading out, well lit, relaxing and quiet. This will minimize distractions and maximize your concentration and ability to focus.

→ **Record important dates.** When you get your syllabi for all of your classes, write down all of the important dates on your calendar. If the instructor changes any test or quiz dates, make sure to note these during the semester. Also record your personal dates and events that are important so you can integrate your study times in with other life priorities.

→ **Create a study plan.** Take a few minutes to outline a study plan to help you stay organized during your study sessions. This will help you organize topics, study notes and the levels of difficulty for the content to be covered. Divide content into sub-sections and set a time limit to spend covering and finishing each one. Keep a note pad with you to write down questions.

→ **Stop daydreaming.** You can physically stand up and turn away from your books to break up the process.

→ **Make room for entertainment, friends and relaxation.** College is more than studying so make sure you have a social life. Also seek out leadership opportunities…it's a great way to acquire soft skills.

→ **Use the "Twofer" concept.** If you are spending time at the laundromat, bring your history notes to study. If you are waiting in line for tickets to the Beyoncé concert, bring your biology flashcards to memorize.

→ **Always make sure you sleep and eat properly.** This is one of the most underrated tips for being successful. It is difficult to do well in class, excel at your job or be successful in your relationships if you are always sleep deprived and do not follow good nutritional habits.

SUBJECT BASED Study Strategies

Here is an example of how to get organized and create a study plan based on the course subject or discipline. For this purpose we will use **HISTORY** as the course content area. With some minor adjustments, you could create a similar plan for English, psychology or biology.

PREP

→ Use a special three ring binder for notes, handouts and assignments

→ Approach history from the perspective of embracing and observing the interesting ways in which the world has changed

→ Daily 30-minute preview:
  - Preview headings, main ideas, graphs, pictures and section summaries/questions
  - Convert headings into questions

DURING THE LECTURE

→ Actively engage, listen and answer as many of your questions as possible

→ Ask questions and discuss concepts and events with your professors

→ Don't forget to confirm and clarify your preview work

→ Don't forget to find the who, what, where, when, why and how

→ Take good notes

AFTER

→ **15 minute Blitz**—Immediately following each class, take 15 minutes to rewrite and review your notes, focusing on:
  - determine the topic and provide an explanation
  - explore the significance/role in history
  - determine what period/set of years does it represent?
  - ask why is this being covered/why is it important?
  - ask what effect does it have on the world today?
  - explain how it affects you personally—what is your opinion of the topic?

→ Write down questions about what was covered during the lecture.

→ Write down unclear content/vocabulary.

→ Always remember, the professor is there to assist your endeavor to learn. Meet with him/her for help or clarification on anything you are unclear about. Test out how he/she feels about your opinion of the event.

Test-Taking **STRATEGIES**

Assessments exist to test your knowledge of a skill or competency in a specific area. Examples of assessments may include tests, papers, presentations or projects. Another example might be demonstrating your knowledge or skills in a clinical environment for areas like dental hygiene or nursing. You may be thinking "I can't wait until I get out of school and never have to take another test!" That would be wonderful, but unfortunately it is not always the case. Many careers require you to continue lifelong learning through continuing education classes, certifications and on-the-job training. Even your performance review at your job is an assessment of how well you have completed the objectives for your job and performed the necessary skills. Learning the most effective "test-taking" skills now will continue to benefit you throughout your life.

Start Preparing Early

Doing well on tests and other assessments starts on day one of class. The instructor may list specifics about tests and assessments in the syllabus along with dates and other key information. Take note of this information. Another early strategy is to create a prep calendar and plan for all of the tests and key assessments that will take place in each of your classes. Be sure to include the following information in your plan:

→ When are the assessments?

→ What information will be assessed each time? Is there a mid-term exam or final? Are they cumulative?

→ How are these assessments structured? Are they true/false or multiple choice, essay or project-based? Will you be working in a group at all? Are you allowed to use any notes? Is there a time limit for the tests? Will you be taking tests online?

→ How will they be graded? Is there a rubric that outlines exactly what the instructor expects in the paper or presentation?

→ Does the instructor have review sessions?

Once you have your prep calendar and plan, here are some additional tips to help you get ready for tests.

→ Review your notes and materials. Do not wait until the last minute. One student recently stated that she tries to review the material she learned that day in class either right after class or later that day. She said just taking the time to do this daily review for 15-20 minutes has turned out to be one of the best strategies she has ever used!

→ Take some time to map out the chapter or information or concepts you are reviewing. Mindmapping can not only be used to take notes, but it can also be used as an effective review tool. We will learn more about this in our note taking section.

→ Teach the material to someone else. While this may happen in a study group, you can also recite the information to yourself in the mirror, to your two-year-old child or to the dog! Knowing you have to teach someone else is one of the best ways to ensure you know the material.

→ Try and predict the test questions. Do you have old quizzes or materials that the test questions may come from? Take some time to go through your notes and predict what the instructors may ask. What did they focus on most in class? Did they give a review or study guide? What did they cover on the PowerPoint or in their lectures?

→ Create a game or use online tools such as Quizlet to help you review. Quizlet is an online study tool where you can make flashcards and review games for yourself. You can also use traditional flashcards to help you review and memorize material.

→ Schedule study time. Remember the time management techniques discussed earlier in this unit. Create a test prep calendar for the parts you plan to study and review each day before the test.

→ Decide in which courses you might benefit from joining a study group or studying with a partner.

→ Clean up your notes or re-write notes after each lecture. Review them every other day.

→ Use the instructor's clues to identify information likely to appear on exams.

Day of the Test or Assessment

Test day has arrived. You have prepared so you feel confident heading into the classroom. Now it is time to practice these additional skills during your assessment.

→ Use positive self-talk. Keep a good attitude and remind yourself that you are going to do your best. It is normal to expect some test anxiety and often a little elevated stress level can drive you to do better. However, it is imperative you are able to manage your anxiety and keep it to a minimum. Relax, breath and channel a PMA (positive mental attitude).

→ Get to class on time. This is not the day to take a new route to school or to try new foods for lunch. Stick to your routine. Eat a well-balanced meal. Don't fill up—just enough to relieve hunger.

→ Make sure you have the proper materials to take the test (paper, extra pen/pencils, calculator, etc.)

→ Read the directions carefully and ask questions if necessary before you get started.

→ Pace yourself. Read each test question carefully and entirely before answering.

→ Build confidence by working on the easier questions first or completing those with the most point value.

→ If you are having trouble remembering answers, skip the question for the time being and come back to it later. Don't forget to come back to it later and never leave a question unanswered.

→ Avoid making random guesses. Eliminate options you know are incorrect in order to make a more educated guess.

→ Try not to second guess yourself unless you are sure you've misread or misinterpreted the question.

→ Stay focused on your test and work until you are finished. Don't worry about classmates finishing before you.

→ When you finish, use spare time to go back over the test to catch mistakes and to review your answers to make sure you have completely answered each question.

Following Up

Sometimes after the test or assessment, we are so glad it is over that we do not consider how to use them as a learning opportunity. Here are some additional tips to help.

→ Evaluate how you did on the test. Did you feel prepared? Do you want to do anything differently for the next test in this specific class? What changes do you plan to make?

→ If your professor goes over the test, make sure to attend the session and pay attention. It is helpful to hear what he/she was looking for as you may be able to use this information on subsequent tests. There also may be times that the instructor will allow points for "corrections," so be sure to take advantage of any of these opportunities.

→ Review your test to see the mistakes you made. Reviewing mistakes and learning from them helps you to prepare for future tests. Also review for errors that the instructor may have made in grading.

→ Read the feedback from the instructor. What specific things did he or she suggest that you can use in future exams? It is also a good idea to meet with the instructor if you have additional questions or if you feel you studied appropriately but did not do as well as you wanted on the exam.

→ Save your tests to study for midterms and final exams. Even if the exact questions aren't repeated, you can learn a lot from the way a professor asks questions.

SURPRISING TIPS FOR TESTS

1. **SCENT ASSOCIATION**
   Study with a distinct smell and carry the smell with you to the test. Make sure it is not a common smell like a perfume that you wear every day or mint.

2. **STUDY BEFORE BEDTIME**
   Get plenty of sleep. Memory is retained during the REM (rapid eye movement) cycles of sleep. The longer you sleep...the more cycles you get.

3. **EAT RIGHT**
   Eat brain foods the day of your test, such as fruits, vegetables and protein. Stay away from carbs and fatty foods that slow your metabolism.

4. **ARRIVE EARLY**
   Get to the test location early, especially if this is a different classroom than you normally meet in. It will help you relieve stress and collect yourself.

5. **CHEW GUM**
   Chewing gum right before the test will increase blood flow to the brain.

While there are many testing and assessments tips that all classes have in common, there are also differences by subject. Here is an example of how to prepare for an English paper or essay.

ENGLISH ASSESSMENT: WRITING A PAPER
Analyze the question or topic and figure out what the instructor is asking you to write about. Remember, in college your professors are not just interested in you summarizing or agreeing, but also in you expressing your opinion and elaborating on the reasons why.
Create a timeline. Break down the sections/topic so you are not writing the entire paper in one night.
Find out if you need to submit a draft or an outline.
Create an outline. Gather your thoughts and resources.
Follow the rubric to ensure you have covered every area and made every edit.
Spell check and proofread for errors before submitting.

MASTERING Your Memory

A significant part of learning is being able to remember or retain what you learned. Here are our top tips for really using your memory to help you become a better student. One thing to consider is that many times you do not want to just memorize material, but you also have to be able to explain, summarize, analyze and evaluate what you have learned. Memorizing and learning the information is just a first step.

 We used one of our Memory techniques (creating an acrostic) to learn the following list. Memory is a **RARE GIFT** and can help you **WIN** as a student!

Repetition. This is a proven way to help you remember things. The more you look at something or re-read it, the more you remember. Back in 5th grade, you likely had to memorize the multiplication tables and take a test on them every week. Doing that over and over sealed it into your brain. Re-read your notes or the chapter on World War II. Say your vocabulary words over and over. You can also use a new textbook or website that might present the information in a slightly different manner. This is another type of "repetition" that can help you learn the material.

Association. Connect to information you already know. The human mind works best in patterns. It continually searches for relationships. No matter how long a thought lies buried, association will often trigger your memory so that you can fully recall long-stored items. Ideas and images do not start independently in the mind, but function more like links in a chain, one after another. This is sometimes called chunking, which is grouping several items of information into one category that's as easy to remember as a single item. The method is effective when you have to learn several new pieces of information at the same time.

Read out loud. There is something about using more than one sense that helps solidify it in your memory. You can read your text out loud, watch a video of the material, or listen to a lecture from class that you have recorded. All of these methods are great ways to help you remember.

Enlist your emotions. Make a personal or emotional connection to the material. If you can find a way to connect what you are learning to something in your personal life, or think of how it makes you feel, this can also help you recall it later. Reliving the moment is when sensory impressions are associated in memory to what you're learning and later help remind you of what you have learned.

Grab a game or tell a story. Use Quizlet, create a Jeopardy game or make up crazy stories with the material—the more elaborate the better!

Invent or use mnemonics. A mnemonic is a strategy or tool that aids in the memorization of information. These memory "tricks" can be in the form of acronyms, acrostics, rhymes or songs.

Find a study partner. Collaborating with others is an effective way to learn material. You can talk it out, quiz each other, compare notes and also review for tests together. They may have picked up some important information that you did not or they may have a way to learn those formulas in math that you have not considered!

Teach it to someone. One of the best ways to see if you know the material is to try and teach it to someone else. Explaining an idea to others requires a deeper understanding. This can be a friend, your baby sister, the dog or even to yourself in the mirror!

Write it down. Writing things down also helps seal them into your memory. Taking notes, rewriting or editing your notes, or summarizing what you have learned are all useful techniques.

Invent a picture or visualization. Think about what you are learning in psychology and try to create a picture in your head. These images can be useful when you try and retrieve the information later.

No cramming. Studies show that if you study the material for a bit and then take a break, it allows time for the material to consolidate in your brain. Breaking things up into smaller pieces allows you to remember better.

The key is to find out what works best for you. Remember memory is a **RARE GIFT** and can help you **WIN** as a student!

MNEMONIC

A mnemonic is a strategy or tool that aids in the memorization of information. These memory "tricks" can be in the form of acronyms, acrostics, rhymes or songs.

ACRONYM

An acronym is a pronounceable word that is formed using the first letters of the words in a phrase. For example, **NASA** stands for **NATIONAL AERONAUTICAL** and **SPACE ADMINISTRATION**.

HOMES

Huron, **O**ntario, **M**ichigan, **E**rie and **S**uperior is a great acronym that helps you remember the five Great Lakes.

ROY G. BIV is an easy way to learn the colors in the rainbow by using an acronym.

R is for **Red**
O is for Orange
is for
G is for **Green**
B is for **Blue**
I is for **Indigo**
V is for **Violet**

ACROSTIC

An acrostic is another type of mnemonic device where you create a sentence made up of the first letters of words you are trying to memorize.

Please Excuse My Dear Aunt Sally ( ) ^ * / + -

Parentheses, **E**xponents, **M**ultiplication, **D**ivision, **A**ddition, and **S**ubtraction
This mnemonic allows us to remember the Order of Operations in math.

My Very Earnest Mother Just Served Us Nine Pickles/Pizzas

Mercury, **V**enus, **E**arth, **M**ars, **J**upiter, **S**aturn, **U**ranus, **N**eptune, and **P**luto
Here we have an easy way to remember the order of the planets from the sun outward.

We Just Like Rushmore

Washington, **J**efferson, **L**incoln, and **R**oosevelt | The American Presidents on Mt. Rushmore

PEG SYSTEM

The peg system is a mnemonic technique for memorizing lists. It works by pre-memorizing a list of words that are easy to associate with the numbers they represent.

For example, memorize these 10 "pegwords" (since they rhyme with the numbers one to 10, it's easy): **one-bun; two-shoe; three-tree; four-door; five-hive; six-sticks; seven-heaven; eight-gate; nine-line; ten-hen**.

Now make up a list of 10 other words and number them. Link each one to the pegword with the same number by means of an image. Suppose your first word is bowl; picture a bun lying inside a bowl. If your second word is desk, picture a shoe parked on a desk. A minute should be enough for all 10.

Note **TAKING**

FORMATS

The format you select for taking effective notes is important as it helps provide organization to the lesson covered in class; allows you to identify the major and minor points, their relationships to each other and concepts; and provides great study guides for review, tests and exams.

→ **Sentence Form** is a series of numbered statements.

→ **Paragraph Form** is considered the easiest but most ineffectively used form in which one writes about an idea until it changes and then begins a new paragraph. Information can be disorganized and thoughts incomplete.

→ **Standard Outline Form** uses Roman numerals to record the main points, alphabet letters for the subheadings, and numbers and indentation to go more in depth organizing information. It can be short or more time consuming if note taking goes into more details.

```
I. Standard Outline
     A. Roman numerals used to record main points
     B. Alphabet used for subheadings
     C. Numbers indentation to go more in depth
          1. can be a short process
          2. more details can make process longer
```

→ **Mind Mapping** is a technique in which you draw a visual diagram mapping the links, sequences and relationships between a main concept or idea using a piece of paper. This method typically features a circle in the middle of the diagram, with the topic, and stems with key points relating to the topic being discussed. One could consider mapping being an easier technique to use when taking notes.

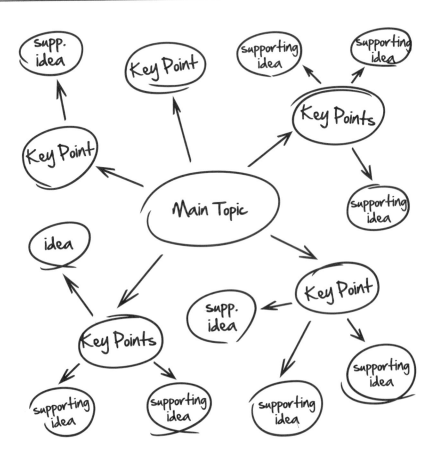

THE CORNELL NOTE TAKING SYSTEM

STEP 1   Prep PRECEDING the lecture

→ Format a sheet of loose leaf notebook paper.

→ Divide the paper into three sections. Use a heavy black marker to draw a dark horizontal line about 1 ½ inches from the top of the page. Draw a dark horizontal line about 3 to 4 inches from the bottom of the page and draw a line about 3 inches from the left side of the paper, from the top to the bottom horizontal lines.

→ The section at the top of the page is the header—where you write the course name, date and topic. The column to the left of the horizontal line is the recall or key words and phrases column. The column to the right of the horizontal line is the record or notes column—where you write the notes about the key words/phrases. At the bottom of the page is the summary section—where you summarize the main ideas of the lecture.

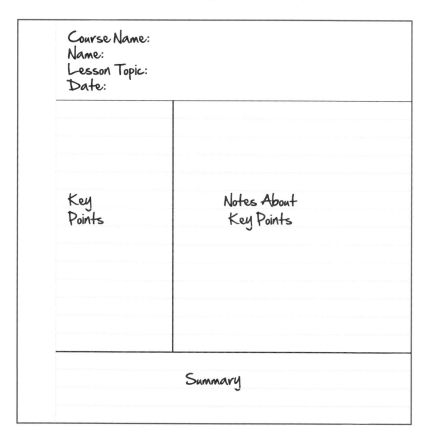

STEP 2   Taking notes DURING the lecture

→ Always record notes legibly so notes are clear and have meaning weeks or months later.

→ Write course name, date and topic at the top of each page.

→ Capture general ideas rather than details to better follow the train of thought or the development of an idea.

→ Skip a line between ideas and topics.

→ Don't use complete sentences. Use abbreviations, when possible. Create and use your own shorthand, such as using "&" for the word "and," but not so many that you can't decipher your notes later.

THE CORNELL NOTE TAKING SYSTEM, cont.

STEP 3 — Review and clarify SUCCEEDING the lecture

➜ Review and consolidate the notes after class as soon as possible.

➜ Read through notes. Make corrections to errors, complete thoughts and fill in the answers to your questions (in the right column); Also pull out main ideas, key points, dates and people (remember these go in the left column); and finish with a summary (at the bottom).

➜ Emphasize the main ideas by underlining or circling the words containing the main ideas.

➜ In the recall or keywords and phrases column, create questions next to the information in the record or notes column. These will be cues for the ideas and facts on the right (in making your recall questions you will be preparing for possible test questions and you will have organized and structured the lecture in a meaningful, easy to remember form).

➜ Study your notes. Now cover up the right side of the sheet, exposing only the recall column. Using your questions, keywords or phrases to help you recall, RECITE aloud the facts or ideas of the lecture as fully as you can. Then uncover the notes and verify what you have said.

➜ Re-read your notes in the right column.

➜ Spend most of your time studying the ideas in the left column and the summary at the bottom. These are the most important ideas and will probably include most of the information you will be tested on.

IN CONCLUSION — Use the 5 Rs

1. **Record** (write) the lecture legibly and always on one side of the paper.
2. **Reduce** the ideas and facts into the recall column.
3. **Recite** the main ideas and facts triggered by your recall phrases.
4. **Reflect** on your understanding of the material.
5. **Review** your notes periodically.

CORNELL NOTE TAKING FOR MATH

The Cornell System can be modified to take notes in math classes. For math you will divide your paper into three columns and record different information in each of the three columns. If necessary, add an additional column to better fit the needs for the material (for example, information learned later in the semester that ties back to this lesson).

→ At the top of the page, write the lesson title, course name and date.

→ Draw lines from top to bottom, dividing the paper into three vertical columns.

→ In the column on the left, record "keywords/rules."

→ Consider adding a "questions" section or column where you write out/clarify the questions you have from your note taking.

Title of Lesson: Course:		Name: Date:
Keywords/Rules	**Problems/Examples**	**Explanations/Descriptions**
Record the formulas, keywords and ideas. Keep the information here brief.	Record each step of the math problems here. Use the (?) symbol next to any step you don't understand.	Record in your own words, the corresponding explanation and/or description for each step of each math problem.

Review and clarify after the lecture

→ As soon as possible following class, highlight titles for "big picture" understanding.

→ Clarify any ambiguous information by meeting with your professor or other students about the information in the textbook.

→ Practice, practice, practice all of the problems and study all of your notes.

→ Do ALL of your homework.

"Persevere! No matter how hard math seems to get, your brain is much more capable, and much more powerful than you could ever believe... push through it. Avoid statements like "I can't do math!" or "When will I ever need this?" as a means of not attempting to learn the material. You can do this. A positive mentality going into a situation will generally yield something positive."

— MARQUIS BROWN, STUDENT, ACA 122-91 SPR. 2016

BE PREPARED for Effective Note Taking

→ Come to class properly rested, alert and ready to engage your best listening skills.

→ Develop a note taking style that is conducive to your learning style.

→ Explore the different note taking methods and decide which will work best for you and for each of your classes.

→ Compare your notes to other students in the class.

→ Note the topic areas that are unclear to you and document your questions. Meet with your professor after class or during his or her office hours to gain clarification.

→ Always read up on the topic your professor will be lecturing on before your class. Familiarity with the topic will help make your note taking easier.

→ Begin preparing for exams from the first day of class by taking effective notes.

USE SYMBOLS and ABBREVIATIONS for Note Taking

Using symbols and abbreviations while taking notes will help. Symbols are especially helpful in math, science and technical content areas. Select one or any combination of these ideas that fit your needs.

SYMBOLS	WORD ASSOCIATED	SYMBOLS	WORD ASSOCIATED
*	important	**	very important
?	question	??	don't understand
=	equal	≠	does not equal
>	greater than	<	less than
&|+	and	/	or
w/	with	w/o	without
b/c	because	vs	against
^	increasing	˅	decreasing
$	costs	#	number

Adapted from **http://www.cpcc.edu/academic_learning/handouts/study-skills-handouts/notetaking/Speed%20 Writing%20in%20Lectures%20Handout.pdf/view**

ADDITIONAL TIPS FOR EFFECTIVE USE OF SYMBOLS AND ABBREVIATIONS

Use parentheses, circles and squares to group information. Indicate important points using underlines and stars. Arrows can be used to connect and link related information.

LISTENING SIGNALS for Note Taking

It is important that you are able to pick up on the verbal and non-verbal cues from your professors when information is important. A rise in your professor's voice or a slight burst of excitement in his or her physical demeanor while lecturing is usually a signal that pertinent information is being shared. Every effective speaker uses signals to telegraph what she/he is communicating. While in class you should expect to receive these signals. For example, she/he may introduce an example with "for example" or "supporting evidence is…"

Signals can be missed by those with poor listening skills. To take effective notes, you must remain alert and ready to receive the information.

COMMON VERBAL SIGNALS

Some common verbal signals include:
- ➔ "There are three reasons why....."
- ➔ "First.....Second.....Third....."
- ➔ "And most important....."
- ➔ "A major development....."

She/he may signal the sending of support material with:
- ➔ "On the other hand....."
- ➔ "Similarly....."
- ➔ "On the contrary....."
- ➔ "In contrast....."
- ➔ "As an example....."
- ➔ "Also....."
- ➔ "Further....."
- ➔ "Furthermore....."
- ➔ "For example....."
- ➔ "For instance....."

She/he may signal a conclusion or summary with:
- ➔ "Therefore....."
- ➔ "Finally....."
- ➔ "In conclusion....."
- ➔ "In summary....."
- ➔ "As a result....."
- ➔ "From this we see....."

She/he may even signal very loud with:
- ➔ "Now this is important....."
- ➔ "Remember that....."
- ➔ "The important idea is that....."
- ➔ "The basic concept here is....."

Quick **TIPS** for Academic Success

1. Go to class. Set the tone of academic success from day one of class. Be there. Pay no attention to the falsehood that it's okay to miss the first day of class because no important work will be covered. On the first day you meet your professor and classmates, find out about the course objectives and the professor's expectations, and ask the professor any questions you have. Class attendance is also an important part of your overall grade in your classes. Missing classes can result in point deduction from your final grade. If you have to miss a class due to illness or an emergency, always contact your professor in advance to arrange submitting homework due on the day you miss and how you can make up work covered in class.

2. Evaluate your progress. Identify your academic weaknesses early so you know the areas in which you might need help and locate the office that can help you. Take the time at the end of every semester to evaluate your progress. This is an opportunity to learn from your successes and from your mistakes. Determine what worked and what didn't work. Revisit your goals to make sure you stay on target. Document the areas that need improving.

3. Reinvent yourself. No matter what type of student you have been in the past, college is a great place to become a new you. If you were introverted, become more outgoing. If you were disorganized, become more focused. College is where you start to become the person you want the world to see.

4. Don't be afraid to ask for help. There are many resources on campus to assist you. Your college wants you to be successful! Reach out to professors and your advisors for help in achieving your educational and career goals. Your success builds their success.

5. Create a time management plan and toolbox that works for you. Everyone has their own system for keeping track of assignments, due dates and other responsibilities. Decide what you want to use and be disciplined about using it. Remember poor time management is one of the biggest obstacles that trip students up so make sure you tackle this as early as possible.

6. Take personal responsibility for your decisions and actions. Be honest with yourself. There will be times when things go well and times when we make mistakes. Admit your mistakes and use them as learning opportunities.

EXERCISE 1.3 | ACADEMIC **READINESS ASSESSMENT**

To be successful in college you need to assess your learning strategies and evaluate your academic skills, determine your strengths and decide how to close any gaps that may hinder your success. The following questions will help you with this process.

1. Based on the information in this section on how adults learn and your learning style, what are some strategies you want to start applying immediately to become a more successful student?

2. Looking at the specific learning strategies below, how would you rate yourself on a scale of 1-5 on each? (5 being high and 1 being low) Based on your results, what changes do you want to make in each of these areas? How can you build on your strengths and then close any gaps?

   a. Test taking skills   _____

   b. Memory skills   _____

   c. Note taking skills   _____

3. One of the key pieces of advice that an admissions counselor at an N.C. university recently gave to prospective students was to stay focused at the community college—focused on your goals and your long-term success. Are you really ready to do this and are you committed to being a successful student? What else do you need to learn about or change to ensure your success?

SELF**DISCOVERY** &
CAREER**EXPLORATION**

IN THIS UNIT:

→ Section 1: Self Assessment

→ Section 2: Researching &
   Evaluating Your Career

→ Section 3: Deciding Your
   Career & Major

→ Section 4: Planning
   & Implementation

"Knowing yourself is the *beginning of all wisdom.*"
—*aristotle*

SECTION 1 | **SELF ASSESSMENT**

IN THIS SECTION:

→ Conduct a Thorough Assessment of Yourself

→ Determine Your Values

→ Identify Your Interests

→ Discover Your Personality

→ Develop Your Skills

SECTION 1 | SELF ASSESSMENT

College is a place where you will discover who you are, what you value, what you want out of life and ultimately who you want to be when you "grow up." This can only be described as a journey of self-discovery and exploration.

Up to this point in your life, there have undoubtedly been many people who have given you career advice or expressed their expectations of you. This advice was probably very beneficial in getting you to where you are today; but now, it is up to you.

→ What do you want?

→ What are your life goals?

→ What career will give you personal and professional satisfaction?

This unit is designed to assist you in the process of choosing your career path and major. To do this, you will employ a simple four-step process of assessing yourself, researching and evaluating career options, making a decision about your career and major, and implementing your career plan.

The first step is to know yourself. A clear, true assessment of who you are promotes self-awareness and will provide a better understanding of yourself and your purpose. Throughout this phase, you will examine your values, interests, personality and skills. This examination can lead to the potential careers you might enjoy pursuing. It will also guide you in choosing the right major for your career and point you toward the prospective colleges where you will continue pursuing your academic goals. Once you discover possible career options, you will research occupation descriptions, required educational training, the skills necessary to be effective in these careers and majors related to your field. After researching career options, you will decide which to pursue and what program/major will best prepare you for this field. The final phase in this process is to establish a plan to implement your career and educational goals.

If you are a student who is returning to school in pursuit of a career reinvention or transition – or maybe an additional degree is needed to advance your career, use this opportunity to re-evaluate yourself and your needs. The self-assessment work you will conduct can also be invaluable to you as you begin to map out a strategy for a transition that aligns with who you are. For whatever reason you have to come to this juncture, this does not have to be an overwhelming experience. The activities in this section will help you explore what options

exist and guide you through the process.

The many ways to assess yourself vary depending on what decisions you have already made and how confident you are about these decisions. Learning about yourself is important, not only in your college and career decisions, but in your relationships with family, friends, instructors and work colleagues as well. Being self-aware takes courage and the ability to see things about yourself you may not like. It also gives you many opportunities to live a life that is deeper, richer and more authentic. It can lead you to a life of fulfillment and purpose.

Check with your community college to see if they offer a career development program for students that can help you make a career decision with the assistance of a trained career counselor. These programs will help you explore and gather information about yourself and careers, so you may make an informed choice about your best career match. You will discuss your goals and expectations, use assessments to generate lists of careers; define your skills, interests and personality; and discover what you are passionate about.

To do a thorough assessment of yourself, you will want to consider the following areas related to your career choice:

→ Values

→ Interests

→ Personality

→ Skills

✥ VALUES

Values are those principles or ideals we hold most dear, the beliefs that are most important to you. Determining your values will help you make effective decisions about your career and about how you want to live your life. For example:

➔ Should you take this new job or stay with your current one?

➔ Should you go into a field where you will be required to travel every week?

➔ Do you thrive on individual achievement and a competitive environment?

➔ Are you okay with working 70 hours a week or will this cause too much personal and family stress?

You may have heard of a game called "Would You Rather?" In this game you have two options or scenarios, and you choose between the two. Giving your response tells us something about what you value or what is important to you. For example, how would you answer the questions below?

1. **Would you rather** be your own boss **OR** work for someone else?
2. **Would you rather** win a prestigious award in your industry **OR** get a 25 percent pay raise?
3. **Would you rather** work on an important project at work **OR** have everyone get along at work?
4. **Would you rather** spend three months going to a job you really hate—for a LOT of money, **OR** do a job for a year that you love for much LESS money?
5. **Would you rather** be able to have a flexible work schedule, including working from home **OR** be able to work in a corporate office with regular travel to other locations of your company?

You can discern important details about your values based on how you answered the questions. If you say you want to be your own boss, then you likely value autonomy and have an entrepreneurial spirit. If you say you would like everyone to get along at work, then you may value harmony and stability in the workplace.

Your values should drive your behavior and your actions. Up to this point, you may have received your values from your parents or other important figures in your life. As a mature, independent person you will want to determine your own values and make decisions based on those values. What others think or what they want you to do may not be as important as they once were.

There are several ways you can identify your values. At the end of these exercises, the questions you want to be able to answer are:

➔ What are my primary values?

➔ What careers will allow me to maintain and employ my values most effectively?

➔ What careers align most with the things I find important to my life?

Listed below you will see two options for identifying your values. Choose one to complete according to your instructor's direction.

Option A | Work Values **SORTER**

Use the College Foundation of North Carolina (CFNC) Work Values Sorter exercise. Go to www.cfnc.org and complete the Work Values Sorter. After completing the assessment, you will be provided with a list of careers that match your values.

1. Log in to www.cfnc.org and create an account or sign in to your existing account.

2. Choose **Plan** then Choose **For Career.**

3. Click **Learn about Yourself** and **Take the Work Values Sorter.**

4. **Complete the chart and questions below** as you view your results.

What were your two main work values?

1. _____ 2. _____

Now review the list of occupations that match your values. Click on the names of the careers and spend some time looking over information about these careers (duties, outlook, required education, salary, etc.). Which careers interest you the most? Enter the information in the table provided below.

CAREER	OUTLOOK	SALARY	REQUIRED EDUCATION

Option B | Discovering Your **VALUES**

This is your chance to really think about who you are and how you want the world to perceive you. Read the questions below carefully and think honestly about your responses to them. Record your responses in spaces provided below. Remember, be honest.

1. Who am I? What do I believe in? What are my values? What are my passions? Use the list below to start discovering your values. Run through the personal values listed and select those that are really important to you.

Achievement	Decisiveness	Helping Society	Money	Responsibility & Accountability
Advancement & Promotion	Democracy	Honesty	Nature	Security
Adventure	Ecological Awareness	Independence	Order (Tranquility, Stability, Conformity)	Self-Respect
Affection (Love & Caring)	Economic Security	Influencing Others	Personal Development	Serenity
Arts	Effectiveness	Inner Harmony	Freedom	Sophistication
Challenging Problems	Efficiency	Integrity	Physical Challenge	Stability
Change & Variety	Ethical Practice	Intellectual Status	Power & Authority	Status
Close Relationships	Excellence	Involvement	Privacy	Supervising Others
Community	Excitement	Job Tranquility	Public Service	Travel
Competence	Fame	Knowledge	Quality of What I Take Part In	Truth
Competition	Fast Living	Leadership	Quality Relationships	Wealth
Cooperation	Financial Gain	Location	Recognition (Respect From Others, Status)	Wisdom
Country	Friendships	Loyalty	Religion	Work With Others
Creativity	Growth	Market Position	Reputation	Working Alone
	Family	Meaningful Work		
	Helping Other People	Merit		

2. Who do I want to be? What do I really want out of my life? What legacy do I want to leave behind?

3. List three things that you love to do. What values are reflected in these activities?

4. Think about your life. What will be most important to you in terms of your quality of life? What things do you want to be able to do?

5. Now summarize your top five values and why you hold those as the most important.

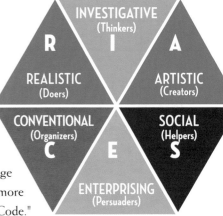

In the mid 1950s, psychologist John Holland developed a theory that people and work environments can be loosely classified into six different groups based on interests. Each of the letters in the Holland Code corresponds to one of the six interests in the graphic to the right: Realistic (R), Investigative (I), Artistic (A), Social (S), Enterprising (E) and Conventional (C). Also known as the RIASEC. Knowing your Holland Code can direct you to particular career fields and college majors. While you may have interests in several of the six areas, you are usually more attracted to two or three of the areas. These two or three letters are your "Holland Code."

HOLLAND Codes

Realistic (Doers)

→ independent, practical, athletic, hands-on, persistent

Prefer: things that are concrete and tangible rather than idealistic

Investigative (Thinkers)

→ analytical, intellectual, methodical, scientific, explorative

Prefer: problem solving and tasks that are scholarly and experimental

Artistic (Creators)

→ creative, intuitive, expressive, sensitive, independent, unstructured

Prefer: authenticity and to work with ideas, abstractions and concepts

Social (Helpers)

→ cooperative, supportive, nurturing, generous, patient, empathetic

Prefer: socializing, helping others, teaching, teamwork, social interaction and relationship building

Enterprising (Persuaders)

→ adventurous, competitive, ambitious, extroverted, persuading, assertive

Prefer: leadership, business, politics, public speaking and taking risks

Conventional (Organizers)

→ detail-oriented, organized, clerical, conscientious, conservative, logical, efficient, thorough, ethical

Prefer: accuracy, practical tasks, quantitative measurements and structured environments

MAJORS Related to the HOLLAND CODES

Here is a list of college majors as they relate to the Holland Codes.

MAJOR:	CODES
Accounting	Conventional
Actuary	Investigative, Conventional and Enterprising
Aerospace/Aeronautical Engineering	Realistic and Investigative
Anthropology/Paleontology	Realistic and Investigative
Architecture	Artistic and Enterprising
Biology	Investigative
Broadcast Journalism	Enterprising and Artistic
Business	Enterprising

List continued on on following page.

MAJORS Related to the HOLLAND CODES

List continued from previous page.

MAJOR:	CODES
Chemistry	Realistic, Investigative and Conventional
Civil Engineering	Realistic
Computer Engineering/Science/Programming	Realistic, Investigative and Conventional
Communications	Social
Criminal Justice	Realistic
Dentistry	Realistic, Investigative and Social
Economics	Investigative, Social and Conventional
Education	Artistic and Social
Educational Administration	Social, Enterprising and Conventional
Engineering	Realistic, Investigative and Conventional
English	Social
Environmental Science	Realistic
Finance	Investigative, Enterprising and Conventional
Fine Arts	Realistic and Artistic
Foreign Languages	Social
Graphic Designer	Realistic, Artistic and Enterprising
Higher Education	Investigative and Social
History	Social
Human Resources	Social, Conventional and Enterprising
Physics	Investigative
Political Science	Social and Enterprising
Pre-Law	Social, Investigative and Enterprising
Pre-Med	Investigative and Social
Psychology	Investigative, Social and Artistic
Public Relations	Artistic and Enterprising
Math	Realistic and Investigative
Music	Realistic, Artistic and Social
Nursing	Realistic, Social, Investigative and Conventional
Sociology	Social
Web Design	Realistic and Artistic
Veterinary Medicine	Realistic, Social and Investigative
Zoology and Wildlife Biology	Realistic and Investigative

You can explore the O*NET website, **www.onetonline.org**, for more information about occupations related to your Holland Code. Click on the "Advanced Search" tab, and then click on "Interests" from the drop-down menu to explore the occupations associated with each Holland type. You can also use the College Foundation of North Carolina's Interest Profiler Exercise on the following page. Two other sites that have Holland Codes linked to careers and majors are: The University of Missouri Career Services site (**http://career.missouri.edu/career-interest-game**) or Purdue University (**https://www.cco.purdue.edu/students/holland.aspx**).

EXERCISE 2.1B | **INTEREST** Profiler

1. Log into **www.cfnc.org** and sign in to your account.

2. Choose **Plan** then Choose **For Career.**

3. Click **Learn about Yourself** and **Take the Interest Profiler.**

4. **Complete the chart and questions below** as you view your results.

What were your two main career interest areas?

1. _____ 2. _____

You will receive a list of occupations that correspond to your interests. Click on the names of the careers and spend some time looking over information about the career (duties, outlook, required education, salary, etc.) Which occupations interest you the most? Enter the information in the table provided below.

CAREER	OUTLOOK	SALARY	REQUIRED EDUCATION

What did you discover about yourself by taking the Interest Profiler?

How do your interests and career goals align?

 PERSONALITY

Making sure there is congruency between your personality and career choice is also essential to ensuring career happiness and success. If you like to be around people and you are sitting at your computer all day, alone, this is not a good match!

In his text "The Pathfinder," Nicholas Lore expresses a concept called the Right Livelihood. This is an ancient Asian philosophical concept that proposes a perfect working relationship and flow between you and the world around you. "Your work fully expresses all aspects of your nature. It fits your innate talents perfectly. It expresses your temperament and personality. It provides the rewards that matter to you. It fulfills your goals. It occurs in an environment that is suitable and appropriate to who you are." (Lore, 1998) It is when you are being you.

Many career development programs offer career assessments, such as the Myers-Briggs Type Indicator® or The Strong Interest Inventory® that explore personality. Each assessment has its own advantages.

PERSONALITY ASSESSMENTS

THE MYERS-BRIGGS TYPE INDICATOR® will identify your personality type and provide a list of career fields people with your personality type often pursue. Katherine Briggs and Isabel Briggs Meyers used the work of Carl Jung to create this tool to help identify one's personality preferences.

DO WHAT YOU ARE® is another assessment that allows you to gain valuable insight into your personality and how and where you may be successful from a career perspective.

TRUE COLORS® is a personality inventory created by Don Lowry. He uses the four colors as a metaphor to translate personality and learning theory into practical information we can apply to our work and our relationships.

EXERCISE 2.1C | Discovering Your **PERSONALITY**

There are numerous ways to discover your personality type. After using the assessment chosen by your community college, answer the questions below. The important thing is to remember that there is not one perfect or "right" type of personality. We are using these tools as a way to discover more about our personalities and how those may inform our career and life choices. Learning about your personality can give insight into the types of activities you find more satisfying and thus point you to particular career fields for more research. Also remember that these assessments are a snapshot and you will want to "validate" the results by asking yourself if this truly describes you. The purpose is to increase your self-awareness so your gut instinct is also an important validation tool.

After completing the assessment, answer the following questions related to your results.

1. What is your personality type? _____
Give a short explanation of your type and characteristics associated with this type.

2. What surprised you about your results? What did you agree or disagree with?

3. Look at the careers that "match" your type. Do any of these careers sound appealing to you? _____
Why or why not?

4. How does your personality type correlate with the career and/or major you are considering at this time?

If your community college does not provide a personality assessment, you can explore more at these sites:
➔ http://www.humanmetrics.com/ (**free assessment**)
➔ http://personalitypage.com/ (for learning more about the types, **no free assessment**)

 SKILLS

When it comes to the importance of candidate skills, employers are looking for leaders who can solve problems, work in a team and communicate effectively. Participation in extracurricular activities has a lot of influence on selection as well. (National Association of Colleges and Employers (NACE) Job Outlook 2015 survey).

You need to have a strong GPA and relevant work experience, but the skills you possess are crucial when looking for a job. Skills can be broken down into two main areas: work content skills and transferable skills.

WORK CONTENT SKILLS are those specific to a particular job or field. They may also be called job specific skills or "hard skills," and are those you need to acquire to show mastery in a particular field. For example, if you are an automotive technician, you need to know the parts of a motor, how to use diagnostic equipment to determine problems with a car and how to repair a transmission or an alternator. If you are a teacher, you need to understand learning theory, how to assess students' progress effectively and how to create a lesson plan. The best way to determine the work content skills needed is to look at a job description or use a resource like O*NET (https://www.onetonline.org/).

TRANSFERABLE SKILLS are those that apply to a variety of jobs and settings. These may be things such as decision making, communication, leadership or teamwork skills. Often these "soft skills" can set you apart and give you a definite competitive advantage in the job market.

Remember that much of your development as a person occurs outside the classroom. Take advantage of programs, opportunities and services offered at your college or in your community to develop your leadership and interpersonal skills. Opportunities to lead or participate in clubs or student government, doing an internship, volunteering or participating in service learning or conducting research are significant ways to develop skills that will not only be beneficial to your career, but also to your success as an individual.

EXERCISE 2.1D | Developing **YOUR SKILLS**

Answer the following questions to do a gap analysis of the skills you possess and those you still need to develop.

1. What skills do you currently have? What are you good at? *You may use the Basic Skills Survey and/or Transferable Skills Checklist at* www.cfnc.org *to complete the table on the following page.*

Basic Skills Survey and Transferable Skills Checklist

1. Log into www.cfnc.org and sign in to your account.
2. Choose **Plan** then Choose **For Career**.
3. Click **Learn about Yourself** and **Take the Basic Skills Survey** and/or the **Transferable Skills Checklist.**

2. Find a copy of a job description you are considering OR look up your career choice on O*NET (https://www.onetonline.org/) and make a list of the skills you will need to be successful in your field.

3. After creating your list from Items 1 and 2 above, complete the chart below with the skills you currently have, those you still need to develop and your plans for acquiring those skills.

SKILLS I POSSESS	SKILLS I NEED TO DEVELOP	OPPORTUNITIES TO DEVELOP MY SKILLS

SECTION 2 | RESEARCHING & EVALUATING YOUR CAREER

IN THIS SECTION:

→ Understand Strategies for Career Research

→ Learn to Conduct an Information Interview

→ Consider Internship and Volunteer Opportunities

SECTION 2 | RESEARCHING & EVALUATING YOUR CAREER

STRATEGIES for Career Research

Now that you have learned about your values, personality, interests and skills, it's time to explore possible career options. A good place to start is with the careers suggested as a result of your self-assessment work in Section 1. Take a look at the industries that interest you, such as education, business, entertainment, STEM, fashion, communications/journalism or healthcare. Then investigate the different jobs and careers related to that industry. It is also important you identify employers by name and type (government, nonprofit, educational institution or corporate).

Once you have chosen the careers to research, make sure you also take time to learn about the current events in our nation and world that are affecting this career. For example, what types of trends are happening in these industries? How is technology impacting them? Is globalization changing the way the jobs are structured?

You can also identify professional organizations and associations related to this field. Is there a group you can join now as a student? The Internet offers a plethora of information about different careers, professional associations, employers, current events and industry trends. This is also a great time to start thinking about people you know who may work in the field you are interested in and begin to make connections with them.

CAREER RESEARCH WEBSITES

The Occupational Outlook Handbook
http://www.bls.gov/ooh/

O*NET
https://www.onetonline.org/

U.S. Department of Labor
http://www.careeronestop.org/

QUESTIONS TO ANSWER
(when researching your career interest)

➔ What are the duties and responsibilities of this career?

➔ What are the required qualifications (skills, degrees, experience)?

➔ What is a normal career path and the employment outlook for this field?

➔ Who are the employers in this field?

➔ What are the professional associations for this field?

➔ What are the most popular geographic locations for this field?

➔ What jobs and companies exist in my current area?

EXERCISE 2.2 | CAREER RESEARCH

Looking back at the career suggestions offered at the end of your assessments, what is one career that really interests you? Investigate the occupation information for your chosen career. Answer the questions below based on what you have learned. You may find more information on the Occupational Outlook Handbook (http://www.bls.gov/ooh/) and the O*NET (https://www.onetonline.org/) websites most useful. Feel free to browse around on the sites and look at other career information, such as the salary links and the career and education planning sites.

What is the career title?	
Provide a brief description for this career.	
What skills are needed for this career?	
What are the minimum education and training requirements? (What degree or program? Also provide examples of "related fields.")	
Is a professional degree required for this career? If so, which one (J.D., M.D., Ph.D., M.A./S.)?	
How many years will the education/degree requirements take? Are you willing to commit?	
What is the salary range?	
What is the job outlook (whether there will be a need for jobs in this field in the future)?	
What are the opportunities for growth and advancement?	
List other sources to pursue for more information related to this field. (This may include resources in the career center and names of local people working in this field; include Internet addresses).	
What other research do you need to do that would help you decide or help you validate your career decision?	

NOW LET'S DIVE A LITTLE DEEPER

Reflecting on your findings for this career, ask yourself:

➔ What are the three most appealing aspects of this career?

➔ What are the downsides to this career?

➔ How does this career align with your interests and values?

➔ Would you still want to do this job if the pay were much less than you desire?

➔ Could you be inspired to work in this field every day?

➔ Do you believe you have the personal qualities and skills to do this work?

➔ Are you willing to commit to completing the formal training and education required to work in this career?

➔ Can you envision yourself being content/fulfilled and successful in this career?

EXPANDING Your Research

Some of the ways to help you select the right career include visiting your campus Career Services and conducting an information interview with someone currently working in your field of interest. You could also pursue an internship or volunteer opportunity in the area you are considering.

VISITING CAREER SERVICES

If you are still having a difficult time defining a career path, seek out the experts for a more extensive exploratory process. As mentioned earlier in this section, career counselors exist to assist you on this journey. A visit with a career counselor can render a more in-depth analysis of your skills, preferences and interests through assessments, activities and reading materials. Take advantage of the one-on-one counseling sessions, career related workshops and online career research databases available to you.

CONDUCTING A CAREER INFORMATION INTERVIEW

A career information interview will give you a realistic view of what it will be like to work in a specific field. It involves identifying individuals currently working in your desired field and asking them questions related to their job. It will help you define a realistic view for your knowledge and understanding of a field.

HOW to Conduct an Information Interview

1. IDENTIFY SOMEONE working in your career field of interest. Be sure to do your research on the company and the individual before you meet with them so you have some knowledge about their career if possible.

2. INITIATE CONTACT. Be sure to use a pleasant and enthusiastic tone.

3. BRIEFLY INTRODUCE YOURSELF, who referred you (if applicable) and explain the purpose of your call.

4. ASK FOR AN APPOINTMENT. Ask if this person has 20-30 minutes to meet, ideally at their workplace to discuss/answer a few questions about their profession. You should assume this person has a busy schedule and not ask to meet on the same day you initiate contact. If they can't grant your request, ask for the name of someone else they might recommend.

5. SEND A FOLLOW-UP EMAIL TO CONFIRM the appointment and honor the agreed upon time to talk and the 20-minute time frame you were granted.

6. THANK THE INTERVIEWEE for their time and send a thank you note.

INTRODUCTORY CALL/EMAIL EXAMPLE

Hello _____, my name is _____ and I'm a student at _____. I am doing some research on the _____ profession and I'm hoping you would grant me an information interview to discuss working in the field. I promise to take up only 20 minutes of your time and I'm willing to come to your office at your convenience. Do you have any availability in your schedule this week or next?

SAMPLE QUESTIONS for an Information Interview

→ What was the reason you decided to enter this field? Was it always your plan or did you happen upon it?

→ How long have you been working in this field and how long did it take you to get to your current position within this company? What jobs or experiences did you have previously?

→ What training or education would you recommend for someone trying to enter this field? Do you have advice on a major and minor for this field?

→ What personal qualities, skills or talents should one possess to be successful in this field?

→ What do you find most rewarding about your job and why?

→ What do you find most challenging in your job and why?

→ What tasks are involved in your typical work day and week?

→ When is the "peak season" in this career? What is a work week like during this time?

→ How does this career fit into/affect your lifestyle?

→ What are the latest changes or trends in the field?

→ What opportunities for growth and advancement exist in the field?

→ What books, websites, professional organizations or other people should I research or talk with?

→ Are there any internships, mentor or shadowing programs within this organization for college students looking to gain experience in the field?

INTERNSHIPS and VOLUNTEER Opportunities

Another way to research is to participate in "real life" activities that help you get a feel for the job and what is it like on a day-to-day basis. You could volunteer in the area you are considering. You may be able to obtain a paid or unpaid internship, or have the opportunity to shadow someone in your field. Another option is Service Learning, a program many schools offer which allows students to become civically engaged while earning a grade related incentive in a course. Check with your community college to see if they offer internships or cooperative education (co-op). Not only do these experiences give you a chance to learn about the working world, but they allow also you to gain valuable real world experience, directly related to your career, that can set you apart from other job candidates. Another advantage is you may create connections with supervisors and colleagues who can be a future reference for you or who can assist you with networking or job opportunities.

It is important that students *take ownership* of their career development. Often many jobs require applicants have some experience before applying, and the Catch 22 is they've spent most of their time earning a degree, leaving little time to gain the experience that is required. For that reason, it is important for students to take advantage of internships, volunteer opportunities and skill development that will enhance their marketability."

Most important, students should always look at every opportunity as a *chance for growth*, even if that opportunity seems remotely outside of their career choice. In an often competitive and diverse workforce, transferrable skills and adaptability are attractive assets to employers. Volunteer experience is also helpful because networking can open doors for potential applicants. Take time to meet influential people, make good impressions and become known to people who can make opportunities available."

— JAMES BASS, ED.D., DIRECTOR OF STUDENT SUCCESS AND STUDENT LEADERSHIP, ROBESON COMMUNITY COLLEGE

You've done a substantial amount of research, exploring and investigating. For some of you, the process has helped you narrow down the list of careers you were considering. For some, you've discovered what you might be good at doing and what you value. Some of you were able to gain a more realistic view about a career you had already chosen. Gathering information can be overwhelming. Try not to put too much pressure on yourself to find the perfect career. Your career selection should not be one choice that will dictate the rest of your life. Instead, allow yourself the flexibility to choose, evaluate and change it if you don't like it. So, approach this experience as if it is just the first step toward a fulfilling career and quality of life.

"My *mission in life* is not merely to survive, but to thrive; and to do so with some passion, some compassion, some humor, and some style."
—*maya angelou*

SECTION 3 | DECIDING YOUR CAREER & MAJOR

IN THIS SECTION:

→ Dispel Myths About College Majors

→ Explore Strategies for Choosing a Career and Major

→ Identify a Parallel Plan

SECTION 3 | DECIDING YOUR CAREER & MAJOR

If the outcome of the career research exercise has supplied you with the right career choice, your next step is to select the major that will train and prepare you to obtain employment in that field. If the research did not satisfy your career decision, try selecting one of the other careers from the lists of suggestions from your assessments and repeat the research process until you find the right fit. If you are having a difficult time deciding between career options, you might find it helpful to refer back to the decision making process in Unit 1.

> A **MAJOR** is a group of courses required by a **COLLEGE** and taken in sequential order to receive a **DEGREE** in a specialized discipline.

Separating Myth From Reality: The "MAJOR" Myth

Most college students think there is a corresponding academic major for each specific career field, and that it's impossible to enter most career fields unless they choose that matching major as a student. This is not true! The reality is the relationship of college majors to career fields varies. Some career choices dictate you choose a specific undergraduate major. However, most college majors don't offer specific preparation for a single type of work. The primary reason students choose the wrong major is so many concentrate exclusively on studying for a specific "job," as if each job required a certain major. Your choice of a major is only one factor in determining your future job prospects and career path.

With some help from Central Piedmont Community College Career Services, we have listed three common myths about choosing a major below.

1. **I should know what my career path will be. I should have a calling.**
   It is perfectly okay if you don't know today what you should major in. That's what this section is all about: the exploration of possibilities. Also, not everyone has a "calling." In many cases the best options when choosing a major is to evaluate your interests, skills and talents. Or chose something you have an organic talent to be successful in doing. One who prefers the outdoors and loves plants might choose a major and career in Horticulture. Or someone who has a fondness for horses might major in Equestrian Studies.

2. **My major will determine my career.**
   In many cases, the career path you choose will direct your choice of a major. For example, if your dream is to become a medical doctor, it would behoove you to select a major that will prepare you for medical school such as Pre-med or Biology. However, there are many examples of majors that prepare you for a broad range of careers. If you major in History, you might be a teacher, work for an art museum, become a lawyer or go into business. Many employers are looking to see that you have completed your degree and that you have leadership and critical thinking skills that can be applied in a number of settings. The path to a career is not always a straight line.

3. **I should pursue a career in a field that has a lot of job openings or money.**
   Choosing a major based solely on the abundance of money or job availability is not wise. You risk choosing a job you hate going to everyday which could compromise your mental, physical and emotional health. There is also the possibility that during the years it takes you to complete your degree, job availability in a market

that has a lot of openings today becomes inundated. This would decrease your job options significantly. Having said that, if there is a high demand for employees in a field that truly interests you…go for it.

STRATEGIES for Choosing a Major

Students often choose their majors unwisely because they lack sufficient information about themselves, potential courses of study, the job market, and how to combine education and career goals.

This is why some self-exploration is necessary. Before you choose your major, you should be asking yourself some key questions. Begin to chart your college career, using your career goals as the basis for decisions about your academic major and minor, elective courses, internships, vacation jobs, leadership commitments and extracurricular activities.

Revisit your self-assessment and career research results. Your self-assessments provided suggestions for possible career paths for individuals that share your interests, values, personality and preferences. This is a great place to start. As you conducted research on possible careers, you probably noticed there were degree requirements or some level of academic training in a related field to prepare for a specific career. These requirements and training are strong possibilities for selecting a major. Always consider flexibility of a major in case you find yourself looking for a different path.

In whatever academic area you decide to major, make sure you assess what else you can do with a degree in that major. There is always the likelihood that job availability or satisfaction is lacking. A flexible degree affords you more alternatives in finding career fulfillment.

Keep in mind that, while researching and evaluating majors, you need to be realistic about what you will be required to do and what you are willing to commit to doing.

The Importance of a PARALLEL PLAN

For many reasons, sometimes a student's plans might not work out. We encourage you to identify a parallel plan (an alternative or back-up plan) for success in addition to planning for your chosen career and major. Interests, circumstances and commitments sometimes change. Majors sometimes require much higher than average GPAs or a high skill level in particular subject areas (like math and sciences) to gain admission into a program. These are a few reasons parallel plans are vital.

For example, let's look at a student's wish to enter a professional career such as becoming a lawyer or a medical doctor. It's a great goal. Most of these programs are highly competitive and accept a limited number of people each year. This makes your academic background especially important for entering these fields. All programs will list a minimum grade point average (GPA); however, the minimum GPA required is usually far lower than the average GPAs actually accepted into these programs. Standardized aptitude tests (MCAT, GRE, LSAT, etc.) are often a requirement. If standardized testing is a challenge for you, it could be a major problem when applying to medical or law school.

NOW LET'S DIVE A LITTLE DEEPER

Regardless of how confident you are your admissions application is competitive or whether you have a 4.0 or a 2.8 GPA, you should have a parallel plan. Any forward thinking individual would have one. Some things to consider are:

➔ Research alternative career options for your major.

➔ If your application into a major or professional program is denied, find out what your application was lacking and make revisions. Refrain from re-submitting a failed application. Ask yourself: Should I take a semester/year off to evaluate how I can improve my credentials, experience, extra-curricular/volunteer work and then reapply?

➔ Many people are accepted when they reapply, especially when they ask the admissions committee what they need to improve and can show evidence of applying what they were told to the new application. So keep trying and continue to build your credentials and qualifications.

➔ Discuss your parallel plan with your career counselor and academic advisor.

EXERCISE 2.3 | **DECIDING** YOUR MAJOR

Considering all of the research you've conducted thus far—your interests, values, personality and skills, answer the following questions related to your major or program of study.

1. What is the career you have chosen? *Occupational Therapy*

2. What will be your college major, concentration and/or minor for your career choice?
Health Science, Associate of Science (bachelor)

3. What are three universities/colleges that offer this major or program?
University of North Carolina -Chapel hill
University of North Carolina -charlotte
East Carolina University

4. Does this major align with your career path and values? ☑ **YES** ☐ **NO**

5. Do you have the intellectual capacity to obtain a degree in this major? ☐ **YES** *maybe* ☐ **NO**

6. Are you willing to commit to the time and effort it will take to complete this major? ☑ **YES** ☐ **NO**

⚹ 7. What else can you do with this major? List at least two alternative career options related to this major. (You can use the site **http://whatcanidowiththismajor.com/major/** for assistance.)

SECTION 4 | **PLANNING & IMPLEMENTATION**

IN THIS SECTION:

→ Create Career and Education Goals

→ Make the Connection to Your Values and Interests

→ Create an Online Professional Presence

→ Maintain Your Portfolio

→ Build Your Network and Professional Brand

"It's not about how you achieve your dreams,
it's about how to lead your life,
...If you lead your life the right way,
the karma will take care of itself, the
dreams will come to you."
—*randy pausch*

SECTION 4 | PLANNING & IMPLEMENTATION

"Motivational author Stephen Covey suggests that college students *'Begin with the end in mind,'* and I think that is a great place to start. It is important for students to have a clear vision for the career that they wish to be in. Doing so will save time and money while attending college."

— JAMES BASS, ED.D., DIRECTOR OF STUDENT SUCCESS AND STUDENT LEADERSHIP, ROBESON COMMUNITY COLLEGE

Begin with THE END IN MIND

Let's step back a minute and reflect on who you are and what legacy you want to leave behind. Imagine you are 90 years old, sitting on a rocking chair on your porch. You are happy and pleased with your life. Looking back on all you've achieved and acquired, all the relationships you've developed; what matters to you most? What would you like to be remembered for?

In his book "The Seven Habits of Highly Effective People," Stephen Covey lists Habit Two as "Begin With the End in Mind." Often we go through life reacting to the things that happen to us and allowing other people to make decisions for us about what is important and what we should do with our lives. We may achieve great things but these can also come at the expense of things that are more valuable to us. Covey says, "If the ladder is not leaning against the right wall, every step we take just gets us to the wrong place faster."

According to Covey, "Begin with the End in Mind" is based on the principle that all things are created twice. There is a mental (first) creation, and a physical (second) creation. (Covey, 1989) The physical creation comes after the mental creation similar to how a building follows a blueprint. You must make a conscious effort to visualize who you are and what you want in life; otherwise you are allowing other people and circumstances to shape you and your life by default. You need to connect to what makes you unique and then define the personal, moral and ethical guidelines within which you can most happily express and fulfill yourself. You can use these guidelines to set your goals, make important decisions in your life and decide how you will use your time, energy and talents.

Now that you have made some important decisions about your values, interests, career and major, it's time to establish your goals. Goal setting is more than simply saying you want to do something or want something to happen. It is the powerful process of envisioning your ideal future and motivating yourself to bring your vision of this future to fruition. It involves you clearly defining exactly what you want to accomplish and for what reason. Your goals help you stay on track and help you reach your mission and purpose in life. Goals drive your behavior and are a reflection of your values. Without a clear definition, your chances of success are reduced considerably.

According to Dave Kohl, professor emeritus at Virginia Tech, creating goals and writing them down is key.

→ 80 percent of Americans say they don't have goals.

→ 16 percent do have goals but don't write them down.

→ Less than 4 percent write down their goals and fewer than 1 percent review them on an ongoing basis.

→ People who regularly write down their goals earn nine times as much over their lifetimes as people who don't.

We've come up with the following **5 Rules of Goal Setting** to help get you started. We believe that following these rules will promote your ability to set realistic goals with confidence and appreciate the satisfaction that will follow, knowing you achieved what you set out to do.

1. **Make sure you set goals that inspire and motivate you.**

2. **Always set SMART goals.**

   Specific → Be clear and well defined.

   Measurable → Be precise with amounts, dates and make sure you can measure your degree of success.

   Attainable → Be realistic. Challenge yourself but be sure to set goals that are possible to achieve.

   Relevant → Make sure the goals are headed in the direction you want your life and career to take.

   Time Specific → Your goals must have a deadline or timeframe to be accomplished.

3. **Put your goals in writing.** Writing them down makes them real. Keep them in a location where you see them every day. This will help keep you focused and remind you of what your intentions are.

4. **Create an action plan.** Making progress toward your ultimate goal requires you write out the individual steps needed then cross each one off as you complete them.

5. **Evaluate and hold yourself accountable.**

GOAL Setting

These questions may help you as you think about your career and educational goals:

→ What questions do you still have about your major that you want to get answered?

→ What questions do you still have about your career?

→ Who do you need to talk to?

→ When do you plan to do these tasks?

MAKING THE CONNECTION to Your Values and Interests

Here is an example of how you can establish academic and career goals while maintaining your values, and interests.

Value: Achievement
Interest: Writing

Possible academic and career goals: I will complete my Associate in Arts degree by May 2018 with no less than a 3.5 GPA, then transfer to the U.N.C. School of Media and Journalism in the fall of 2018. I will pursue a career at a newspaper, magazine or online literary source.

During the exercise at the end of this section, you will practice writing your goals. Using the research you have conducted, you will establish one long-term goal, two mid-term and two short-term goals that support and are directly related to your career plan. For the purpose of this exercise, try focusing on your academic and career goals.

→ **A long-term goal** is a goal to be accomplished in five or more years and should be related to your career.

→ **A mid-term goal** can be accomplished in one to five years and should be related to the education/work experience that will help prepare you for this career.

→ **A short-term goal** can be accomplished in one year or less and should be related to your semester here at the community college or your next semester.

→ Don't forget to make them **S.M.A.R.T.**

CHANGING Job Market

Development is a lifelong process. You will always be working on your career plans, even long after you get your degree. You will want to consider how to adapt to the changing job market, learn how to create an online presence and develop your networking strategy.

Because job markets will be much more competitive when you finish your degree, you should think about going beyond your major. Here are some suggestions:

→ Develop skills that are immediately useful to the employer through leadership opportunities outside the classroom. Plan to gain additional experience through summer or part-time work, intern/externships, volunteer experience, extracurricular activities and elective courses.

→ Become competitive in today's market by obtaining the experience and competencies related to your chosen field. Review job announcements for the professional attributes companies look for in prospective employees. Pay attention to the job duties, responsibilities, the preferred experience and training. This will help you build soft skills and competencies needed in the field.

→ Begin researching companies/organizations in your field of interest. Observe how they rank in the competitive market. Evaluate which fit in with your life and employment needs.

→ Supplement your degree with work experience and elective coursework to support your career goals.

→ Consider combining your liberal arts degree with solid technical skills.

→ Avoid premature commitment to a field you don't yet understand or single-minded concentration on one area of knowledge to the exclusion of other areas not yet discovered.

→ Make your degree marketable by choosing a school with a solid reputation and excellent career placement services for their graduates.

→ Use LinkedIn to see the types of jobs alumni from your school are doing. This is also a good way to network.

Creating a Solid Online **PROFESSIONAL PROFILE** or **PORTFOLIO**

In today's market, social and professional networking sites have become essential resources for career research, personal connections and staying current in your industry. Professional recruiters utilize them as additional avenues to search for and assess potentially employable candidates. What does your online image say about you? If an employer were to Google your name, what would they see? What would your online presence tell them about you?

An online profile or portfolio is a structured collection of information housed on the Internet that demonstrates your talents, skills, abilities, achievements, experiences and training. The purpose is to provide an organized relevant showcase of your professional existence. In today's competitive job market, a creative and informative online presence could be the key to setting you apart from other candidates.

Why an Online Profile or Portfolio is **IMPORTANT**

- ➔ Companies use the sites to seek out new talent.
- ➔ Students from all majors can adapt and utilize an online profile as an effective tool for marketing themselves to prospective employers.
- ➔ It's a great introduction tool to the professional world.
- ➔ Creates a way to establish and maintain a strong online image.
- ➔ Demonstrates your ability to stay relevant and compete in a tech-driven society.
- ➔ Contains concrete evidence of your talent, skills and abilities.
- ➔ A solid selection of professional work samples can prove to employers you have the expertise to do the job.
- ➔ The basic concepts can be adapted to enhance your marketability in almost any field.

The **FOUR STAGES** of Designing Your Online Profile and Portfolio

STAGE 1 — Assess Your Talents and Skills

Review your skills, abilities and past experience to determine what you have to offer an employer. How do your skills relate to a possible employer's needs and required qualifications for the jobs in which you are interested?

STAGE 2 — Research the Options and Find Your Fit

Once you identify what skills and abilities you need to showcase to prospective employers, you are ready to find the online networking sites to illustrate these capabilities. Research the different professional websites and decide which is the "best fit" for your career goals. Pay close attention to site popularity. Know which sites are frequented most by employers and which have the strongest capability to house and showcase the most impressive presentation of your information. A couple of great sites to start with are www.linkedin.com and www.weebly.com.

STAGE 3 — Create and Design

Once you select the organizational Web format that will best illustrate your professional attributes and accomplishments, it's time to create your professional profile. Begin with a student profile. Be creative and tasteful. Make sure your design is conducive to your target audience and professional field. Research what prospective employers are looking for and incorporate it in your design. Consider prioritizing your portfolio according to the skills and experiences that are most directly related to your career field. The key to your organizational format is easy access. Use the tab pages and/or headers to categorize the materials.

Don't be surprised if an employer asks to review your online profile before granting an interview. Some employers Google you to see if your online image aligns with company culture and image.

Use strong visuals to demonstrate the success of your work, accomplishments and connections to the community. Upload videos, images and articles to make your profile engaging.

STAGE 4 — Review Your Portfolio and Make It Go Live

Know your portfolio inside and out. Have a professional critique your profile. Proof it for proper and correct grammatical use. When you go to an interview you want to be able to use your portfolio to illustrate your skills and abilities. Employers and users need to be able to access the information they are seeking quickly. Once you have made revisions and proofread it, make it go live.

The **COMPONENTS** of an Online Portfolio

1. **Identifying Documents**
   a. Résumé
   b. References (get permission and use privacy settings) and letters of recommendation
   c. Career plan/professional summary
   d. Academic transcripts (if appropriate and grades are an asset)
   e. A graduation photo of your degree or of you displaying your degree
   f. Licensure, professional certification

2. **Achievements and Honors**
   a. Certificates of completion for professional and academic training
   b. Honors, awards, grants, scholarships, Dean's List recognition
   c. Certificates of appreciation
   d. Articles
   e. Letters of commendation

3. **Work examples**
   a. Examples of your abilities as they apply to your field. Use college experiences, class projects, internships, practica, etc. Faculty can help you decide the most appropriate material to include.
   b. Photos must always have proper resolution.
   c. Journalism/public relations: make sure your written pieces are uniformly presented.
   d. Healthcare fields such as nursing: examples of care plans, research interests, etc.
   e. Business, education and leisure fields: examples of projects, lesson plans, research reviews and case studies are appropriate.
   f. Drawings and designs, flyers
   g. Links to articles, pictures of events, programs and trainings you were responsible for creating, designing, facilitating or planning.

4. **Leadership, Volunteer Service and Civic Engagement**
   a. Leadership/service transcripts (positions held, years of service, projects and committees chaired)
   b. Written event timelines, newsletters, samples of written minutes and anything created to improve functionality (such as electronic financial ledger)
   c. Leadership awards and honors (Who's Who, student leader of the year, service awards, etc.)
   d. Publicity samples, flyers
   e. Training workshops attended and facilitated; positive evaluations
   f. Newspaper reviews/articles

Maintaining Your **PORTFOLIO**

Whatever electronic/software format you choose, remember to display the samples in a way that shows off your creativity, skills and abilities.

➔ Be prepared to change your profile/portfolio when trends change by replacing irrelevant or dated information with new pieces or adding/creating new ones. Rearranging and prioritizing the content might also be necessary.

➔ Use caption/title pages to categorize information on the site.

➔ Insert titled divider tabs/pages to separate each sample category included in the portfolio.

➔ Position all work samples in the same direction, so the interviewer will not have to continually rotate visuals.

➔ Avoid political and/or religious materials.

➔ If possible display a chronological order of your work to showcase your strengths and key accomplishments.

➔ Never have blank or unfinished pages on your site.

in. Building Your NETWORK and PROFESSIONAL BRAND

Networking is an important skill that will not only help you get your first job out of college, but it will also be useful to you throughout your career. You will want to maintain your network forever! Another key element of career building is thinking about yourself as a brand. Just like Nike, Apple and Coca-Cola have a specific and recognizable brand, you do as well. Anytime someone interacts with you in person, online, via phone or in an email, you are projecting your brand. Think strongly about what brand you are communicating and if you need to make any changes to your "messages." Here are some ideas for networking and brand management:

→ **Connect** with classmates, co-workers, professors, professional contacts and mentors. Stay updated with your connections and build new professional contacts as often as you can. Research which professional networking sites are most frequented and respected. Decide which parallel best with your professional image and needs.

→ **Set up a LinkedIn professional profile.** Be sure you have a separate professional and social presence. Facebook and Twitter can be used for your social presence. LinkedIn also has a "Student Jobs" site (www.linkedin.com/studentjobs) which posts internships and jobs for students and recent graduates.

→ **Visit and update your profile regularly** with new developments and changes in your professional life. Always remember to thank those who endorse your skills and respond to messages.

→ **Participate in industry-specific blogs and discussion boards.** Look for industry associations, organizations and groups to join in your field. Career Services and your professors are a great place to start. Utilize Internet resources to find these professional associations, organizations and groups. Utilize the profiles of people you respect in your chosen field. Make them a part of your network and be an active participant.

→ **Google yourself.** You need to know what a prospective employer might see when they Google you. This can be a positive or a negative, so you want to maintain a positive online presence.

Did You Know?

A 2014 survey from CareerBuilder found that 51 percent of employers who research job candidates on social media said they've found content that caused them to not hire the candidate. However, one third (33 percent) of employers who research candidates on social networking sites say they've found content that made them more likely to hire a candidate. (www.Careerbuilder.com; this survey was conducted online within the U.S. by Harris Poll on behalf of CareerBuilder)

→ **Be aware of who you share your site with and how they are representing you online.** Inappropriate content posted by others may be seen on your site. Monitor friends' pictures, "tags," and other content. Control who sees your information online by using privacy settings.

→ **Be careful what you post on blogs.** Your social views and political opinions may not be acceptable to potential employers.

EXERCISE 2.4A | CAREER & EDUCATION **PLAN**

This is a chance to summarize what you have learned from this unit and incorporate your learning into your career and educational goals. Answer the following questions in paragraph format and then complete your goals and action plan following.

1. What did you discover about your interests, values, personality and skills? How do these items align or point you to a particular career or field of work? Name the career and discuss how you found your "match."

2. What did you learn from your Career Research project? After researching the specifics of your career, are you still interested in your first choice or have you changed your mind based on any of your research? How well does this occupation you have chosen mesh with the type of lifestyle you want to live?

3. What is your parallel plan? If something happens in this first career choice, what is your second choice and how will you get prepared for this second option?

4. What is one other thing you need to do in terms of furthering your research? How can you test your ideas?

EXERCISE 2.4B | CAREER & EDUCATION **GOALS**

Using the research you have conducted, establish one long-term goal, two mid-term goals and two short-term goals that support and are directly related to your career plan. For the purpose of this exercise, be sure to focus on your academic and career goals.

Long-term Goal: Name your career goal.

1. _____

Mid-term Goals: Name your four-year degree or other academic related goals.

1. _____

_____

2. _____

_____

Short-term Goals: Name your community college or transfer related goals.

1. _____

_____

2. _____

_____

Quick **TIPS**

1. Be true to yourself. Now is the time to take a minute and ask yourself some deep personal questions about what you want out of your life and how college can help you achieve your goals. Remember to tell yourself the truth.

2. Take advantage of the Career Development resources offered at your community college. Check to see what types of programs or assessments you can take. Make an appointment with a career counselor to discuss your career options and what majors will be applicable to that career choice.

3. Do extensive research about the career and major you are considering. What is the job outlook for this career? Do you know how long it takes to get the degree you need? Make sure you are well informed and willing to commit what it takes to accomplish this goal.

4. Remember you do not have to be 100 percent certain of your major to choose your college but it does help. Knowing your major will help you choose the right college and the right program, which can save you time and money in the long run.

5. Set career and educational goals based on the decisions you have made at this time. You will want to revisit these periodically to make sure you are on track or to make any changes based on new information or decisions you are making.

6. Create a career strategy. Make sure to include how you want to be perceived professionally and what your brand says about you. Create a network and keep it up to date at all times. Learn how to write a résumé and interview effectively. Continue to build your skills and learn new things. All of these things will ensure you have value in the marketplace.

7. Supplement your degree with a strong set of soft skills. Seek opportunities outside the classroom to sharpen your competencies in oral and written communication, collaboration and teamwork, critical thinking and creative problem solving, professionalism and work ethic.

8. Remember that life is all about change. Companies change and go out of business. New technology requires we learn new skills. Things may happen in your personal life to change your plans. This is okay. Life is about being able to adapt.

These are the tasks/steps you can take toward accomplishing your goals. Examples of tasks are provided in grey below. Write down your top 4-5 tasks that will help you achieve your goals above. Be as specific as possible.

ITEM	PLAN/DESCRIPTION	START DATE	DEADLINE	NOTES
Associate's Degree	Complete 24 credits	Fall 17	Summer 18	
Contact transfer university	Find out requirements Arrange campus visit			
Apply to university				
Shadow a professional				
Research internship opportunities				

NOTES

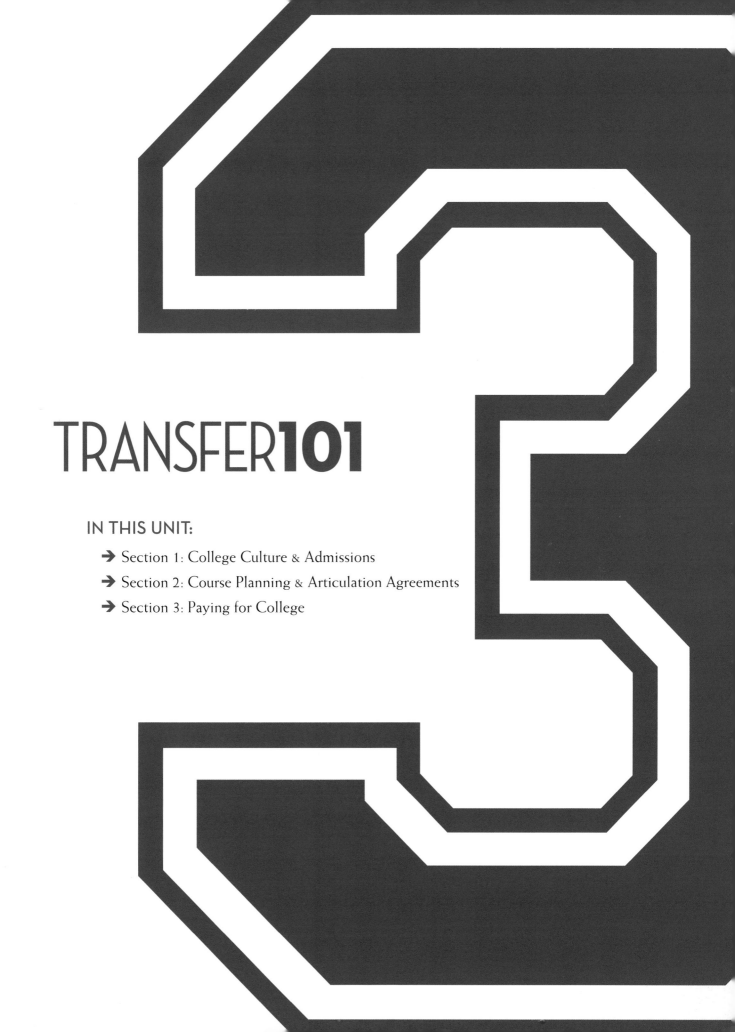

TRANSFER**101**

IN THIS UNIT:

→ Section 1: College Culture & Admissions

→ Section 2: Course Planning & Articulation Agreements

→ Section 3: Paying for College

SECTION 1 | COLLEGE CULTURE & ADMISSIONS

IN THIS SECTION:

→ Research Different Types of Colleges and Universities

→ Explore Your Individual College Needs

→ Investigate the Best Colleges for Your Career and Major

→ Research the College Admissions Process and Requirements

→ Complete a Transfer Admissions Plan

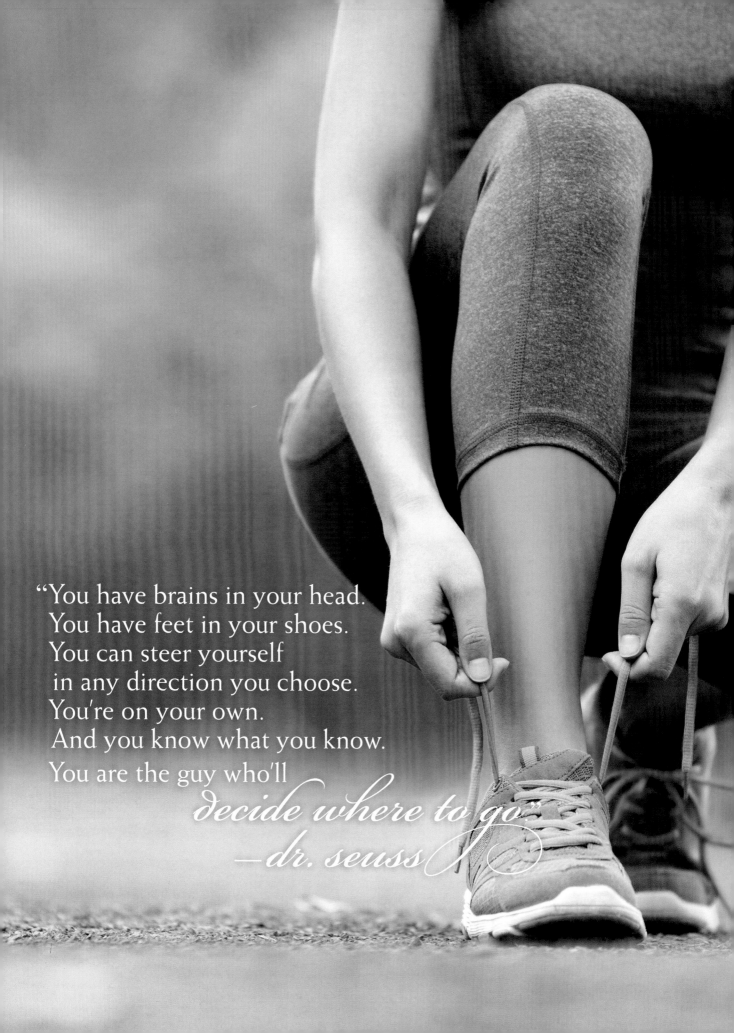

"You have brains in your head.
You have feet in your shoes.
You can steer yourself
in any direction you choose.
You're on your own.
And you know what you know.
You are the guy who'll
decide where to go."
—dr. seuss

COLLEGE CULTURE & ADMISSIONS

Congratulations! You have chosen your program/major and now you are ready to choose the four-year college or university to which you will transfer in order to complete your bachelor's degree. There are so many decisions and options in front of you! Should you go to a school near your home? Should you go to a public or private university? Would you prefer a large or small campus? In this chapter you will explore the different varieties of colleges and universities that exist in the United States. Then you will select the top three universities for your individual and academic needs.

College culture can be described as the combination of academic focus, language, behavior, values, philosophy and outlook that are part of a college education. It is the unspoken "rules" that college students learn to fit into a college environment. College cultures differ depending on the campus, but there are some similarities.

The first the first thing you should know about college culture is the difference in the learning ideologies from what you experienced as a youth. As mentioned earlier in unit 1 section 3, pedagogy refers to the art and science of teaching children. The art and science of helping adults learn is called andragogy.

At the ACA Conference: Networking for Student Success in the fall of 2015, presenters held an "Inside Information" University Admissions Panel. Attendees gained valuable insights and learned tips that will benefit students planning to transfer to North Carolina universities. These appear throughout this section. Universities represented on the panel included U.N.C. Charlotte, U.N.C. Wilmington, East Carolina University, Queens University, Appalachian State University, North Carolina Central University, and Western Carolina University.

As you begin to think about your college choices and the admissions processes/requirements for those colleges, consider these tips provided by the university panel when asked the question, "What is the #1 tip you would give to community college students planning to transfer to your specific university?" Here's what the panel guests had to say:

TOP TIPS FROM N.C. UNIVERSITY ADMISSIONS COUNSELORS

1. Apply early.

2. Stay focused at your community college.

3. Connect early with transfer admissions at the university or in your program area.

4. Know how many credit hours you need to transfer, what GPA is required and research the program of study.

5. Be proactive.

6. Visit the schools.

7. Be your own best advocate!

8. Check your e-mail!

The **DIFFERENT TYPES** of **COLLEGES** in the United States

One of your current tasks is figuring out which college is the best fit for your individual, financial and career needs. In the spirit of andragogy you will be taking a close look at your personal needs and directing yourself in making decisions about which college environment you will choose. Size, location, campus culture and cost are just a few of the factors to consider in making such a decision. Let's explore the different types of college environments that exist.

Public Colleges/Universities

→ Funded by local and state governments

→ Lower tuition for in-state students

Examples: University of North Carolina-Chapel Hill, University of North Carolina-Charlotte, North Carolina State University, North Carolina Central University

Private Colleges/Universities

→ Selective admission

→ Funded by private sector

→ Not administered by local, state or national government

Examples: Queens University, Wake Forest University

Universities

→ Larger and offer more majors and degree options (B.S./A; M.S./A; Ph.D.)

→ Most universities contain several smaller colleges

→ May have to apply for admission into a specific college within the university in addition to general admission

→ Students can prepare for many types of careers or for further study in graduate school

→ May be public or private

Examples: Appalachian State University, East Carolina University

Liberal Arts Colleges

→ Most are private and focus on undergraduates

→ Typically offer four-year programs leading to bachelor's degree

→ Majors include literature, philosophy, history, languages, mathematics, humanities, and social and natural sciences

→ First two years consist of general education courses; then designate and complete major course work

Examples: Wingate University, Davidson College, High Point University

Community Colleges

→ Two-year colleges offering associate degrees and certifications that focus on career readiness

→ Can also prepare you to transfer to a university for a bachelor's degree

→ Often an affordable and convenient option

Examples: Central Piedmont Community College, Wake Tech Community College, Robeson Community College

Vocational-Technical & Career Colleges

→ Offers specialized training to students who are interested in a particular industry or career

→ Not required to take general education classes in all subjects

→ Certificate of completion or an associate degree

Examples: Paul Mitchell School of Cosmetology, NASCAR Technical Institute

Online Colleges

→ Majority of classes offered online

→ Convenience of taking class from home

→ May require more coursework to compensate for not physically attending the class in person

Examples: University of Phoenix, Capella University, Liberty University Online

Ivy League

→ Often viewed by the public as some of the most prestigious universities worldwide; consistently ranked among the top 15 universities in the U.S.

→ Associated with academic excellence, selectivity in admissions, social elitism, and large endowments

Examples: Brown University, Princeton University, University of Pennsylvania, Yale University

Arts Colleges

→ Focus on the arts

→ Provide training in, for example, photography, music, theater or fashion design

→ Most usually offer associate or bachelor's degrees in fine arts or a specialized field

Examples: California College of the Arts, Art Institute, Savannah College of Art and Design

Men's/Women's Colleges

→ Specifically for men or for women

→ Historically, many U.S. colleges were gender-segregated (until late 1860s)

→ Liberal arts, private and focus is on undergrad studies

Examples: Meredith College (Raleigh), Trinity University, Wellesley, Morehouse College, Hampden-Sydney College

Religiously Affiliated

→ Affiliated with a religious faith

→ Usually private

→ Curriculum may or may not be dictated by the religious affiliation

Examples: St. Andrews Presbyterian College, University of Notre Dame

Special Interests

→ Campus population focused on a specific type of student or area of interest

Examples: Gallaudet University (for the deaf and hard of hearing), Military institutions (U.S. Naval Academy, Virginia Military Institute)

Historically Black Colleges/Universities (HBCUS)

→ Student population majority is African American

→ Programs, services & activities relevant to African American students

Examples: Johnson C. Smith University, Winston-Salem State University

Hispanic Serving

→ 25% full-time population is made up of Hispanic students

Examples: Arizona Western College, Valencia College (FL)

As you can see, there are many options to choose from in considering which college is the best fit for your individual needs. The challenge is for you to be truthful about what your needs are, not what others believe is right for you or what the most popular choice might be. Statistics have shown that choosing the right college has a significant impact on your success as a student and your motivation to complete your degree.

Here are some additional aspects to consider when you are thinking about the type of college you would like to attend.

COST

- How much can you afford to spend on college?
- Do you plan to work while attending college?
- Does the school offer scholarships and generous financial aid?

LOCATION

- Do you want to be in a city or rural area?
- What geographic area do you prefer? Do you want to travel to a different part of the country?
- Do you want to be near family or friends?

MAJOR/PROGRAM

- Is this college known for having a strong reputation in your major?

- Is it likely that you will pursue graduate study after completing your undergraduate program? Do you want to look at a school that offers your graduate program as well?

- Do you need classes offered online or in the evenings?

CAMPUS SIZE

- Will you be comfortable at a large university or smaller one?

- What is the student-to-faculty ratio and average class size?

- Do you want to recognize everyone on campus or have the opportunity to interact with many different people?

FACULTY/STUDENT SUPPORT

- Do you want to do research with the faculty in your major?

- Do you prefer a school where you can get to know the faculty vs. being in larger classes?

- What types of internships, study abroad, job placement and academic support services does the school offer?

CAMPUS LIFE

- Is participating in Greek Life, other organizations/clubs or activities important to you?

- Do you want to attend a school with a diverse population?

- What type of meal plans and food options are available on campus and nearby?

HOUSING

- Will you live on campus, with your parents, or in an off-campus apartment?

- Does the school guarantee housing for transfer students?

- Are there learning communities offered in which students can live together in housing dedicated to their majors/programs, study needs (Quiet Housing), academic honors (Honor Student Housing) or organization interests (Fraternity/Sorority Housing)?

The ADMISSIONS PROCESS

The next step in the admissions process is to create a Transfer Admissions Plan. Part of that plan is knowing what the admission requirements are for your chosen colleges. Your Transfer Admissions Plan requires you to research each university, document your findings and create a tracking system. This will assist you with adhering to all deadlines for admissions and financial aid.

After interviewing admissions counselors and other professionals from more than 20 different North Carolina colleges and universities, we have created a list of the Top 10 Tips to consider as you begin the admissions process. Before you start your Transfer Admissions Plan, review the following tips and consider how they might make your admissions journey more successful.

10 Ways to Tackle College Admissions

1. Visit the top two or three campuses you are interested in attending. One of the biggest mistakes students make is not visiting a college campus before attending. Don't plan to make your final college selection without visiting at least your top two or three choices. How serious are you about choosing the best college for yourself?

Sign up for a tour of the campus and ask if you can attend a class. Always take along another pair of eyes and ears and ask as many questions as possible about the college, the atmosphere and the classes. There is nothing like the gut feeling you have when you walk around the campus and talk with individuals at the school. Refer to the Preparing for Your College Visit checklist on page 114 for more ideas.

2. Conduct an information interview with a member of the faculty or admissions to learn more about academic life at this college. Some questions to consider include: What is the average class size? Are faculty teaching courses in my major or are they being taught by graduate students? Are faculty members accessible and supportive? What types of counseling, tutoring and career services support are provided here? Does the college offer any special orientation or transition support for transfer students?

3. Talk to graduates of the colleges you are considering. Ask what made them choose this college. Did it prepare them adequately for their careers? What would they do differently today? Would they recommend this college's program to an individual pursuing your career path?

4. Evaluate how successful you will be at this college. Ask yourself: Why are you going to college? Keep asking yourself this question. How will this specific school help you build your future and maximize opportunities in your career? Are you prepared for the academic rigor and requirements to graduate? Does the college offer opportunities for extracurricular activities that support your growth as a student and community member? Can you see yourself thriving in this environment and graduating from this university?

5. Consider your finances. Create a plan of how you will pay for your education. Have you applied for all financial aid and scholarships that are available? Does the college have any special scholarships for transfer students? Do you plan to live on campus? Will you be working while in college? Are there any on campus work study programs available? Planning realistically now will contribute to your ability to make more well informed final decisions later.

6. Remember that application deadlines are not suggestions. Whether it's for admissions, SAT or ACT registration, financial aid, scholarships, or campus housing, never miss the deadlines. Missing deadlines will likely have negative results. Create a calendar and adhere strictly to all deadlines. Get organized by creating a file for each college you are applying to (See To Organize Your Search on p. 114). Be prepared for the workload of completing your applications and gather all the documents you will need.

7. Start saving early for application fees. This is often an overlooked step. You do not want to miss a deadline due to lack of funds for the application. The average application fee for colleges in the United States is approximately $41. Keep in mind that there are many schools that will waive the fee for students with financial need, while others might offer a waiver to students who apply online. (U.S. News and World Report)

8. Make sure you know exactly what is required for the admission packet. What type of application must be submitted? Will you be required to apply to the college of your major in addition to general admission to the university? Do you need transcripts from your community college or high school? Is an essay required? Do you need references or letters of recommendation? Plan early (See Summarizing Your Findings p. 123-124).

9. Talk to your community college professors or academic advisors about which colleges may be a good fit for you. Choose one or two faculty members who may be able to write a letter or recommendation for you if needed. The faculty member should know you well enough to speak about your academic record, specific examples of how you performed in class and about your motivation and character. Be sure to follow up with deadline reminders to anyone you ask for a recommendation.

10. When making your final choice, seek the advice of family and counselors about where you should apply. Discuss your college options with those who know you well and whose opinion you value. They can help you sort through the options and give you different perspectives.

Checklist for **PREPARING FOR A COLLEGE VISIT**

You would not buy a car without test driving it, right? You also do not want to select a college without first visiting the campus, if at all possible. Here is a list of things to consider when you are visiting colleges.

BEFORE YOU GO

☐ Check out the college's website and take a virtual tour.

☐ Set up an information session and formal tour by visiting the college website and signing up.

☐ Make a list of questions you want to get answered while you are there from either admissions counselors, students or faculty.

☐ Find out if you can visit an actual class. Many colleges will allow this if you plan in advance.

☐ Find out if your particular area of study has a special information session. For example, the business school may have a separate information session for prospective majors.

☐ Research the school along with student and parent comments on sites such as College Navigator, UNIGO, College Board, etc. You may find information here about what students like or dislike about the school. Remember this is a sample of information and not everyone's opinion!

WHILE YOU ARE THERE

☐ Find out about housing. What are the options for transfer students? When is the deadline for housing? How are roommates chosen?

☐ Ask to see a classroom. Even if you cannot attend an actual class, often the tours will take you by a classroom or auditorium where lectures are held.

☐ Ask about the career services and job placement process. This is very important. Do they offer internships for their students? What percentage of students move into a job right after graduation?

☐ Find out about campus life and activities available for students. What types of clubs and organizations do they have for students to be involved in? Do they have intramural or club sports? Do they have an orientation for transfer students? All of these activities will help you assimilate faster as a transfer student.

☐ Ask about advising. Who does the advising? What is the process for registration?

☐ Talk with students about their experiences. If you take a tour, ask the guides any questions you may have. What do they like best? What do they dislike? Have they felt supported by the university? Do they feel the campus is safe?

☐ Ask about financial aid and scholarships and any deadlines you need to work toward.

☐ Ask any other questions related to admissions for which you still need answers, such as deadlines, requirements, and notification timelines.

AFTER YOU RETURN

☐ Take some time to "rate" your visit. What did you like best? What questions do you still have?

☐ Talk with your family and friends about your visit.

☐ If you met with any faculty or admissions representatives, follow up your visit with an e-mail or note thanking them for their time.

Getting Started with **YOUR ADMISSIONS PROCESS**

Let's say you've decided to apply to five colleges/universities. Three of the five are your top choices and two are back-up colleges just in case your top choices don't work out. Just remember that the application process can be taxing as well as exhausting. In some cases the admissions processes are designed this way to weed out those without the intellectual savvy and organizational skills to navigate their way through the process. Be sure that you develop a well-organized search and application process. This will save you time and frustration as well as help you make the right decision about where to transfer.

ORGANIZE YOUR SEARCH

→ Create an electronic folder for each college to which you plan to apply.

→ Create a sub folder for each of the following—application, references, financial aid, transcripts, essays, housing and contacts.

→ Make sure that you include a check list of tasks with the correct dates and deadlines.

→ Update files every time you complete a task.

→ Always have a back-up copy of everything.

First you need to figure out what type of application you are required to submit and what deadlines apply. Some colleges use the common application (**www.commonapp.org**) and some schools have specific school applications. The **Common Applications** is an undergraduate college admission application through which applicants may apply for admission to over 600 colleges and universities in the United States and abroad. More than 800,000 students submitted 3.45 million applications through the Common App last year. Check to see if your school requires the Common Application or they have their own **College Specific Application**. Make sure you also understand what the deadlines are. Do they have one fixed deadline or do they have rolling admissions? Rolling admissions is an open timeframe where you may be able to apply throughout the year.

Regardless of the type of application you use, here are some tips to completing those documents.

➔ Make sure that you have proofread and have run spellcheck on all of your information before you submit your application.

➔ Use a secure computer to protect sensitive and confidential information.

➔ Don't leave any blanks on the application—enter N/A for non-applicable when a question does not apply.

➔ Protect and keep track of all passwords.

➔ Try to finish the application in one sitting and use high speed internet connection.

➔ Always print a hard copy of the application for your personal files.

➔ Read through the entire application before you click submit.

➔ Print and save a copy of the confirmation that your application has been received.

➔ Once filed, check your email daily for college communications—follow directions and deadlines to the letter.

➔ Make sure that you have respectable email addresses and voicemail messages on your phones.

Another key item to research prior to starting your process is the scope of the admission requirements. Do you need to write an essay? Do you need letters of recommendation? Make sure you note carefully that transfer student admission requirements are often very different than those for applying to college as a freshman. For example, many schools do not require an essay or SAT/ACT scores for transfer students if you meet the minimum course credit requirement (24-30 credits). However, if you do not meet the minimum course requirements, you may have to apply as a freshman. Do your research on the school's website or talk with a transfer admissions counselor to make certain.

TRANSCRIPTS

You will be required to submit official copies of your transcripts to each college you apply to for admission. This means that you'll need to make a formal request to all of your former schools—any community or four-year colleges at which you have taken classes, and possibly even your high school transcripts. Do not leave any college transcripts out for any reason. Admissions will consider this a red flag if they realize you did not include transcripts from a prior school. Be honest in this process.

• Find out how the college defines the term "Official Transcripts." This usually means sealed with the college's official seal.

• Find out whether transcripts must be sent directly from the college to the admissions office or attached to a transcript form.

• Check the number of transcripts required from each school.

• Always check to make sure that the admissions office has received your official copy.

LETTERS OF RECOMMENDATION

• Use former community college professors who can attest to your level of commitment and academic performance. Advisors for your civic/leadership engagements are strong references as well.

• Get permission from your references to use them and provide all of your all pertinent information and deadlines.

• Make sure you give the references enough time to complete and submit your request. Also, send a reminder one week before the deadline.

• Always send a thank you to your references.

ESSAYS

Many times when you have completed the minimum course requirement for transfer to a four-year college/university, there is no essay requirement for admission. However, you may come across a college that does require one. Admissions essays are a very important piece of the admissions process. These are an opportunity for you to show off your skills, strengths and talents.

Most colleges want to know how attending their college will benefit you and play an active role in your career and life goals. You may also have a chance to tell your unique story and motivation to pursue your career interests. This is a good opportunity for you to explain any special circumstances/issues in your academic past. For example: why you had low grades at an earlier time in college or why you dropped classes during the middle of the semester.

Make sure that when you are writing your admissions essay, you maintain your integrity. Be authentic and true to who you are.

When it comes down to the final decision on where to apply, more than anything else, you should be yourself throughout the admissions and selection process. Think about your passion and what drives you. Show who you are and how you will contribute to the learning community at the university. Colleges want to have a variety of students from different backgrounds and varied experiences.

Remember, your application is not complete until the admissions department has received everything. Contact the college directly to ensure your application is complete once you have submitted it.

ADMISSIONS ESSAY WRITING TIPS

➔ Attend a writing workshop.

➔ Brainstorm ideas and create an outline before you begin the essay.

➔ Open with a strong statement.

➔ Always give examples that support your positions and prove your points.

➔ Conclude your essay by summarizing your opening and body then state your conclusion.

➔ Have a community college advisor proof your work and give you feedback.

➔ Read it out loud to yourself.

➔ State how your major at this college will help you reach career and life goals.

➔ If necessary, show evidence of grade improvements.

Quick **TIPS**

1. Cast a wide net. It's perfectly okay to have a favorite or first choice for your transfer college, but choose at least five to seven other colleges to investigate as well. If you don't get into your first choice, it's always good to have a back-up plan. Don't make the mistake of only applying to your first choice and then missing out on other opportunities due to deadlines and unmet requirements.

2. Be unafraid to apply to "dream" colleges. You might be surprised. At the same time, apply to at least three colleges which are highly likely to admit you. Be sure to choose "safety" schools you would be happy to attend. These may be considered "safety" schools due to their cost.

3. Look into colleges that you know little or nothing about. It's a good idea to research at least two or three colleges you know little or nothing about but offer the major that interests you. Read student reviews and news articles about the colleges you are considering. It is sometimes a good idea to look outside your comfort zone.

4. Avoid choosing a college based on where your friends go. One of the worst reasons to choose a college is because your friends go there. You can plan to visit your friends during breaks and vacations.

5. Avoid choosing a college based on your favorite athletic team. A great football team doesn't necessarily mean a great academic program. We like to follow the teams we grew up rooting for, but your priority when choosing a college should be academic and career related. Don't equate educational quality with name recognition.

6. Investigate for yourself. Separate reality from baseless opinions. "Hard to get into," "party school," or "too expensive" for someone else doesn't necessarily mean the same for you. Don't accept generalizations without evidence. Do your research.

7. Don't rule out all colleges early because of cost. Many colleges offer scholarships, financial aid, tuition installment plans, and student work programs that make them far more affordable. Make sure you research all financial aid options and speak to a counselor so you are well prepared for deadlines and applications that need to be completed.

8. Don't put all your eggs in one basket. The College Board states that students should apply to five to eight institutions, including a range of options from safety schools (colleges students are positive they'll get into) to reach schools, those where admissions may be more of a stretch for some students.

9. Schedule a campus visit. Remember, being in the physical campus environment can be the best way to get a feel for the school and decide if it is right for you.

10. Ask questions. You can talk to alumni, your professors and friends, students currently at the college and admissions officers. Talk to as many people as you can about the college options you are considering. This will help you make the most informed decision.

11. Make sure you know and understand the admission requirements. Create a file for each school and make sure you are observing all deadlines. Also give yourself plenty of time to submit a strong application. Don't force a rushed application because you waited to begin them until the deadlines were upon you.

12. Make sure you have a backup plan. Apply to more than one school so you can ensure you have alternative options if needed, just in case your first choice doesn't work out.

EXERCISE 3.1A | COLLEGE CULTURE **EVALUATION**

In this exercise, you will analyze and determine what characteristics of a college/university are most appealing to your individual needs. This worksheet will help you discover the best college for you based on what you value and consider most important.

TABLE 1

For this activity, consider what you have learned about college culture so far. Use the table below to help you decide what cultural factors of a college campus you prefer. Select one of the factors listed on each row.

TYPE OF COLLEGE CULTURE			
	Large university	Small college	
	Public	Private	
	Co-ed	Men's/women's	
	Traditional	Online/evening	
	Big metropolitan location	Small town location	
	Ethnically diverse	Minority serving	
	In-state	Out-of-state	

TABLE 2

Use the table to list and rank the factors related to your personal college needs. You can refer back to the questions in this chapter on pages 111-112 to think through each category.

FACTORS	RANK
Cost	1.
Location	2.
Major/Program	3.
Size	4.
Faculty/student support	5.
Campus life	6.
Housing	7.

Based on the preferences you selected in tables 1 and 2, you should have a general idea of what you are looking for in a transfer college. Visit www.collegeboard.org to explore a more detailed search of the different colleges/universities that meet your needs as transfer options. List three colleges that you would consider attending below.

A: _____

B: _____

C: _____

TABLE 3

In the table below, enter your score on a scale of 0-5 (5 being the best fit and 0 being no fit) to judge each feature for each school listed. Consider each feature by asking yourself, "Am I comfortable with this feature of the school?" or "Do I like this feature of the school?" When evaluating factual information, such as "Is my major offered?" enter a 5 for yes and 0 for no.

SAMPLE QUALITIES:	College A	College B	College C
University Name: *Fill these in based on the answers you wrote for Table 3*			
Solid reputation for my major or program			
Distance from home			
Campus size			
Diversity/ethnic make-up			
Average # of years to graduate			
City/town size and makeup			
Cost			
Reputable faculty and research opportunities			
Career preparation/internships/ job market network			
What do my instincts tell me?			
Fill in another personal quality that you must have on your campus: *(Examples would be fraternity/sorority, has a learning community I am interested in, has great food options, etc)*			
1.			
2.			
TOTAL SCHOOL VALUE:			

Based on your finding, rank your top three college choices.

1: _____

2: _____

3: _____

Keep in mind that this exercise is to help guide you in the decision making process. It is not an absolute test for choosing which college you should attend.

EXERCISE 3.1B | **TRANSFER ADMISSIONS** PLAN

Your College Transfer Admissions Plan is a systematic process of proactive activities and actions for the purpose of gaining admission into the four-year college/university you desire. It can also be considered your marketing plan. For the purpose of this class you will be designing your own individual transfer admissions plan.

PART 1 | **ADMISSIONS RESEARCH**

As part of your overall transfer admissions plan, you will be researching your top two colleges. You may start with online research at the school's website for some of the questions and then confirm or go into more detail as needed by speaking personally to someone from the college. You may choose to interview an admissions counselor or ask these questions when you make one of your campus visits. How you gather the information is up to you.

Listed below are questions to research. Feel free to add additional questions based on your personal needs and interests.

The name of the university being researched is: _____

GENERAL INFORMATION AND CAMPUS LIFE

1. Describe the college culture of this university.

2. What major will I pursue at this university? Is this major accredited?

3. How many credits are required to transfer? (minimum and maximum)

4. If I stay on target to graduate or complete the minimum credits at my community college, how long will it take me to graduate from this university?

5. What are three benefits to attending this university?

6. What is campus life like?

7. What is the demographic break-down of the student population? (Example demographics can include ethnicity, gender, international population, etc.)

8. Is this a residential campus? Can transfer students live on campus?

9. What is the average class size for my major? Are classes in my major taught by faculty or graduate assistants?

10. What are some ways in which this college maintains strong connections with the workforce and community?

11. What sources of financial aid are available to transfer students? Are there any special scholarships for transfer students?

ADMISSIONS REQUIREMENTS

1. How much is the application fee?

2. What type of application must be submitted (the college's specific application, the Common App, etc.)?

ADMISSIONS REQUIREMENTS cont.

3. What transcripts are required?

4. Are references or recommendation letters required? (How many?)

5. Is an essay required? (What is the essay topic?)

6. Is an interview required or recommended? Is this in person or via phone? Is this with an individual or panel?

7. Is the application deadline fixed or rolling? If fixed, list the actual deadline.

8. What's the minimum GPA requirement? What's the competitive GPA?

9. Are there additional requirements to be accepted into my major?

10. Do I need an SAT/ACT score for admission? What is the competitive score?

PART 2 | **SUMMARIZING YOUR FINDINGS**

This is where you will compile and track your admissions progress for each university to which you apply.

First Choice

Name of college:	Location:
Major/minor:	Cost per year:
Contact:	Login/password:

Admissions Requirements

ITEM	REQUIRED Y/N	DEADLINE/FEE	COMPLETED Y/N	CONFIRMED/ UNIVERSITY RECEIVED
Application (cost, electronic, paper)				
Test scores (number of copies)				
Official transcripts (number of copies)				
References/ recommendation letters				
Admission essay (topic)				
Personal interview (personal, phone)				
Campus housing application				
Financial aid application				
Scholarship applications				
GPA requirement (list minimum and competitive)				
Credits required (what is the minimum number of credits required?)				
Notes/special instructions				
Admission decision (accepted, wait-listed, denied)				

PART 2 | **SUMMARIZING YOUR FINDINGS** cont.

Second Choice

Name of college:	Location:
Major/minor:	Cost per year:
Contact:	Login/password:

Admissions Requirements

ITEM	REQUIRED Y/N	DEADLINE/FEE	COMPLETED Y/N	CONFIRMED/ UNIVERSITY RECEIVED
Application (cost, electronic, paper)				
Test scores (number of copies)				
Official transcripts (number of copies)				
References/ recommendation letters				
Admission essay (topic)				
Personal interview (personal, phone)				
Campus housing application				
Financial aid application				
Scholarship applications				
GPA requirement (list minimum and competitive)				
Credits required (what is the minimum number of credits required?)				
Notes/special instructions				
Admission decision (accepted, wait-listed, denied)				

PART 3 | **NEXT STEPS/ACTION PLAN**

Now that you have researched all of the requirements for admission to your intended colleges, let's plan your next steps.

1. What questions do you still have about the colleges you are considering?

2. Based on everything you have learned about college culture and admissions, what are two steps you can take within the next 3-6 months to ensure your transfer admissions plan will be successful?

3. Create a task list and action plan of the steps you need to take to ensure you meet the deadlines for college admission.

ACTIONS	TARGET DATE	NOTES	COMPLETE/ INCOMPLETE

Go confidently in the direction of your dreams. Live the life you have imagined."

—*henry david thoreau*

SECTION 2 | COURSE PLANNING & ARTICULATION AGREEMENTS

IN THIS SECTION:

→ Investigate Degree Requirements

→ Learn About Course Planning and the Transfer Articulation Agreements

→ Complete Your Program Evaluation and Degree Checklist

SECTION 2 | COURSE PLANNING & ARTICULATION AGREEMENTS

In previous chapters you researched the educational requirements for your career and selected the major that will best prepare you for that career. Now it's time to take a realistic look at pursuing the course requirements for a degree in your chosen major.

One of the most significant things you will learn during this course is the importance of course planning and progression to your successful transfer to a four-year college. Course planning and progression refers to the sequence of course work a student must take in order to satisfy the academic requirements of an intended degree.

Course Planning is **IMPORTANT** Because

→ It provides a clear view of the academic requirements needed to receive a degree.

→ It helps you establish academic goals with a realistic date for completion.

→ It allows one to evenly balance out the course workload each semester.

The concept of successful course planning is dependent on many things. Some of the most vital are being discussed in this chapter. In fact, there are three very important steps to successful course planning.

Examining what formal academic training, certification and/or credentialing is required will include gaining an understanding of:

→ how course requirements relate to and vary based on your major and intended degree.

→ what major or degree program will best prepare you for a career in that field.

→ which courses you must take to fulfill the requirements for that major.

→ what different types of college degrees exist (see table below).

TYPE OF DEGREE:	DESCRIPTION	COMMON MAJORS	ADMISSION REQUIREMENTS
Certification	A designation earned by a person to assure qualification to perform a job or task.	Certified public accountant, licensed personal counselor, registered nurse, teaching, welding	Dependent on degree earned, exam scores, and experience
Associate's (A.A., A.S., AE)	Consists of general education courses and usually takes two years to complete.	Majors vary depending on program interests. Arts, fine arts, science, graphic design, welding, HVAC, nursing	May have open admissions; high school diploma required
Bachelor's (B.A., B.S.)	Undergraduate studies. Four-year degree considered the entry level degree for several fields and will have academic major attached to it.	Business, English, biology, chemistry, sociology, pre–law, engineering, education, pre-med	Dependent on school and major; GPA, Scholastic Assessment Test (SAT) score
Master's (M.A., M.S., M.B.A.)	Granted to individuals who have undergone study demonstrating a mastery or high-order overview of a specific field of study or area of professional practice. Post-undergraduate level course work. Usually takes two or three years to complete.	Counseling, social work, business, psychology, student affairs for higher ed	Dependent on bachelor's major, GPA, Graduate Record Examinations (GRE) scores, and master's program
Doctor of Philosophy (Ph.D.)	Usually based on at least three years of graduate study and a dissertation; the highest collegiate degree obtainable.	History, higher ed administration, mathematics, biology	Dependent on bachelor's major, GPA, Graduate Record Examinations (GRE) scores, and Ph.D. program

Knowing what a college catalog is and how to use it encompasses:

→ being knowledgeable of the academic jargon.

→ understanding how to read and comprehend course descriptions and progression.

Keeping up with the academic terminology on the collegiate level can be challenging. Following is a list of some of the jargon you will hear throughout your college experience. It is also important to note that these terms may be different in other states.

TERMS You Should Know

MAJOR: The area of academic study in which the student focuses or concentrates. There are required courses that must be taken in order to receive a degree in a major.

MAJOR CONCENTRATION: A focus within a major. For example, a student might choose to major in business administration with a finance concentration.

MINOR: The secondary field of study. It must be different from the major and it requires the student to take fewer credits. Some universities have requirements for acceptance into the minor program.

TRANSFERABLE COURSES: College level courses that will transfer to a four-year college or university. Depending on the course and the four-year college's course requirements, transferable courses may or may not fulfill the general course requirements. This means that the course may only count as an elective toward your major.

GENERAL EDUCATION COURSES: The basic courses required for a four-year degree. These courses usually include some English, math, science, humanities and foreign languages. The number of credits required for each of these will vary depending on the college.

ELECTIVE COURSES: Courses that will count as elective credits toward graduation at a four-year college. These courses are not required for a major but can support another area related to your major.

PART-TIME AND FULL-TIME COURSE LOAD: This refers to the number of credit hours a student takes during a semester. Your full- or part-time status as a student directly affects the number of years it may take you to complete your degree. The number of credits required for part- or full-time status varies depending on the college. A full-time college course load is usually nine to eighteen credit hours.

OPEN MAJOR: A common major at the college/university into which a student is automatically admitted into upon admittance to the university. Some common majors include English, history and political science.

CLOSED OR COMPETITIVE MAJOR: Students must apply for acceptance into the intended major in addition to general admission to the university. Applying to the major program usually involves adhering to additional academic requirements as well.

TERMINAL DEGREE: The highest degree obtainable for a major.

PRE-PROFESSIONAL PROGRAMS: Careers that require a post undergraduate degree. Examples include law, medicine, dentistry, etc.

SHC: Semester Hours of Credit which refers to the number of hours per week a student is in class during a semester. (Also referred to as hours or credit hours)

Understanding How to Use a College Catalog and Read a Course Description

Every college has a catalog that describes academic programs, student services, policies and procedures. The publication also describes all classes offered by the college. An example of a course description is listed below. Course descriptions also note if there are pre-requisite courses that are required before one is able to take the desired course.

ENG 111. Writing and Inquiry. 3.0 Credits. Class-3.0. Clinical-0.0. Lab-0.0. Work-0.0
This course is designed to develop the ability to produce clear writing in a variety of genres and formats using a recursive process. Emphasis includes inquiry, analysis, effective use of rhetorical strategies, thesis development, audience awareness, and revision. Upon completion, students should be able to produce unified, coherent, well-developed essays using standard written English.

STEP 3 — Evaluating the academic course requirements for the college of your choice

Understand the course requirements for your chosen major at the university and the correlation to the general education requirements at your community college, which include:

→ what type of degree you are pursuing.

→ what transfer degree you should be enrolled in at the community college in order to transfer to a four-year college/university.

→ how the Comprehensive Articulation Agreement works between your community college and your four-year university.

→ what general education classes you need to take while at the community college.

→ how many credit hours are required for graduation with an associate or bachelor degree.

→ if your major at a four-year college is open or closed.

→ in which area of the college/university your major is housed.

→ what is the terminal degree for your major.

Knowing the course requirements for your intended degree will help you plan out the courses you need to be taking at a community college which will transfer to the four-year college of your choice. It is important to make sure you are on the right path by enrolling in a college transfer associate's degree. This degree is designed for students who plan to transfer to four-year colleges and universities and fulfills general education requirements. Transfer degrees include the Associate in Arts and Associate in Science. The degree you choose should be determined by your intended major at the university.

Transfer Degree Majors

ASSOCIATE IN ARTS	ASSOCIATE IN SCIENCE
EDUCATION	PRE-MEDICINE
BUSINESS	BIOLOGY
ENGLISH	CHEMISTRY
HISTORY	COMPUTER SCIENCE
LIBERAL ARTS	MATH
(College courses comprising the arts, humanities, and natural and social sciences)	

College Transfer/Articulation AGREEMENTS
THE COMPREHENSIVE ARTICULATION AGREEMENT (CAA)

The Comprehensive Articulation Agreement (CAA) applies to all 58 North Carolina community colleges and all 16 constituent institutions of the University of North Carolina.

The CAA is applicable to all North Carolina community college students who successfully complete a course designated as transferable, or graduate with an A.A. or A.S. degree and transfer to a constituent institution of The University of North Carolina. The regulations for implementation of the CAA were originally approved by the Board of Governors and the State Board of Community Colleges.

The revision of CAA policies and curricula is designed to better facilitate the original purpose of the CAA: to optimize the transfer of credits between the institutions of the North Carolina Community College System and the University of North Carolina institutions. The focus of the current review of the CAA includes the following:

1. **SUPPORTING** current general education requirements at four-year institutions.

2. **ESTABLISHING** a process for maintaining currency.

3. **ENSURING** current information is universally accessible to students and advisors at both four-year institutions and community colleges.

4. **EACH UNIVERSAL** General Education Transfer Component (UGETC) course transfers for lower division general education equivalency.

5. **HIGHLY STRUCTURED** Universal General Education Transfer Component (UGETC) guaranteed transferability to U.N.C. four-year institutions.

6. **UNIVERSITIES' PUBLISHED** four-year degree plans which identify community college courses that provide pathways to degree completion.

The revised Comprehensive Articulation Agreement serves as a current and adaptive agreement that supports more students completing both the associate and baccalaureate degrees.

Eligibility

To be eligible for the transfer of credits under the CAA, the student must graduate from the community college with an Associate in Arts (A.A.) or Associate in Science (A.S.) degree and have an overall Grade Point Average (GPA) of at least 2.0 on a 4.0 scale and a grade of "C" or better in all CAA courses. Students who do not complete the degree are eligible to transfer credits on a course-by course basis.

THE 16 CONSTITUENT INSTITUTIONS OF THE UNIVERSITY OF NORTH CAROLINA

Appalachian State University

East Carolina University

Elizabeth City State University

Fayetteville State University

North Carolina A&T University

North Carolina Central University

North Carolina School of the Arts

North Carolina State University

University of North Carolina at Asheville

University of North Carolina at Chapel Hill

University of North Carolina at Charlotte

University of North Carolina at Greensboro

University of North Carolina at Pembroke

University of North Carolina at Wilmington

Western Carolina University

Winston-Salem State University

Benefits of Completing Your **ASSOCIATE'S DEGREE** Before Transferring

→ The CAA enables North Carolina community college graduates of two-year Associate in Arts (A.A.) and Associate in Science (A.S.) degree programs who are admitted to constituent institutions of the University of North Carolina to transfer with junior status.

→ Universities cannot place requirements on students transferring under the CAA that are not required of their native students.

→ A student who completes the Associate in Arts or Associate in Science degree prior to transfer to a U.N.C. institution will have fulfilled the U.N.C. institution's lower-division general education requirements.

→ Due to degree requirements in some majors, additional courses at the U.N.C. institution may be required beyond the general education courses and pre-major courses taken at the community college.

→ Community college graduates of the Associate in Arts or Associate in Science degree programs who have earned 60 semester hours in approved transfer courses with a grade of "C" or better and an overall GPA of at least 2.0 on a 4.0 scale will receive at least 60 semester hours of academic credit upon admission to a U.N.C. institution.

→ Requirements for admission to some major programs may require additional pre-specialty courses beyond the pre-major taken at the community college. Students entering such programs may need more than two academic years of course work to complete the baccalaureate degree, depending on requirements of the program.

→ All courses approved for transfer in the CAA are designated as fulfilling general education or pre-major/elective requirements. While general education and pre-major courses may also be used as electives, elective courses may not be used to fulfill general education requirements.

→ CAA courses taken beyond the 60-61 SHC of credit in which the student received less than a "C" will not negate the provisions of the CAA.

Comprehensive Articulation Agreement between The University of North Carolina and The North Carolina Community College System
http://www.nccommunitycolleges.edu/academic-programs/college-transferarticulation-agreements/comprehensive-articulation-agreement-caa

Transfer Assured Admissions Policy (TAAP)

The TAAP assures admission to one of the 16 U.N.C. institutions under the following conditions:

→ Admission is not assured to a specific campus or specific program or major.

→ Students must have graduated from a North Carolina community college with an Associate in Arts or Associate in Science degree.

→ Students must meet all requirements of the CAA.

→ Students must have an overall GPA of at least 2.0 on a 4.0 scale, as calculated by the college from which they graduated, and a grade of "C" or better in all CAA courses.

→ Students must be academically eligible for re-admission to the last institution attended.

→ Students must meet judicial requirements of the institution to which they apply.

→ Students must meet all application requirements at the receiving institution, including the submission of all required documentation by stated deadlines.

If a student is denied admission to a U.N.C. institution, then he or she will be notified in writing by the institution. In this notification, the student will be directed to the College Foundation of North Carolina (CFNC) website (www.cfnc.org) where the student will be given information regarding space availability and contacts in the respective U.N.C. Admissions offices. It is the student's responsibility to contact each institution's admissions office to get specific information about admissions and available majors.

If the previous steps do not result in admission to a U.N.C. institution, then the student should contact the CFNC Resource Center at 1-866-866-CFNC.

Transferring **WITHOUT** Completing an Associate's Degree

Although it is beneficial to complete a degree before transferring, it is not required. You can complete between 24-30 transferable credits at a North Carolina community college and be eligible for transfer admission at a university. Note that these credits need to be in specific courses to meet the minimum course requirements (MCR) for admission. Students will need to contact the transfer university to understand the specific requirements. If you are not enrolled in an associate's program you should meet with an academic advisor, faculty advisor or guidance counselor to discuss your transfer options in more detail.

GENERAL EDUCATION Courses and **PRE-MAJOR** Courses

The Associate in Arts (A.A.) and Associate in Science (A.S.) degree programs in the North Carolina Community College System require a total of 60 or 61 semester hours credit for graduation and are transferable to any U.N.C. institution. The overall total is comprised of both lower-division general education and pre-major courses. This curriculum reflects the distribution of discipline areas commonly included in institution-wide, lower-division general education requirements for the baccalaureate degree.

The Associate in Arts (A.A.) and Associate in Science (A.S.) degree programs include general education requirements that represent the fundamental foundation for success and include study in the areas of English composition, communications, humanities and fine arts, natural sciences and mathematics, and social and behavioral sciences. Within these discipline areas, community colleges must include opportunities for the achievement of competence in reading, writing, oral communication, fundamental mathematical skills, and basic computer use. Students must meet the receiving university's foreign language and/or health and physical education requirements, if applicable, prior to or after transfer to the four-year institution.

The **A.A.** and **A.S.** degree programs of study are structured to include two cotmponents:

1. Universal General Education Transfer Component (UGETC) are the courses that transfer for lower division general education equivalency as part of the new CAA and comprises a minimum of 30 semester hours of credit, and

2. Additional general education, pre-major, and elective courses which prepare students for successful transfer into selected majors at U.N.C. institutions and bring the total number of hours in the degree programs to 60-61 semester hours.

N.C. COMPREHENSIVE ARTICULATION AGREEMENT (CAA)
60-61 Semester Hours of Credit (SHC) for Transfer Degree

45 SHC General Education
- → 31-34 Semester Hours of Universal General Education Transfer Component (UGETC), plus
- → 11-14 additional Semester Hours of General Education courses selected from the Transfer Course list

15 Semester Hours of Pre-Major Courses

ASSOCIATE IN ARTS	ASSOCIATE IN SCIENCE
ENGLISH - 6 (SHC)	ENGLISH - 6 (SHC)
HUMANITIES/ARTS – 9 (SHC)	HUMANITIES/ARTS – 6 (SHC)
SOCIAL/BEHAVIORAL SCIENCE – 9 (SHC)	SOCIAL/BEHAVIORAL SCIENCE – 6 (SHC)
MATHEMATICS – 3-4 (SHC)	MATHEMATICS – 8 (SHC)
NATURAL SCIENCE – 4 (SHC)	NATURAL SCIENCE – 8 (SHC)
ADDITIONAL GEC – 13-14 (SHC)	ADDITIONAL GEC – 11 (SHC)
OTHER REQUIRED HOURS – 14 (SHC)	OTHER REQUIRED HOURS – 14 (SHC)
ACA 122 – 1 (SHC)	ACA 122 – 1 (SHC)

For a complete list of transfer courses visit: http://www.nccommunitycolleges.edu/academic-programs/college-transferarticulation-agreements/comprehensive-articulation-agreement-caa

In addition to the Comprehensive Articulation Agreement (CAA), there are other agreements in N.C. specific to particular programs and an agreement with the independent colleges in N.C. Here is a summary of those agreements.

Uniform Articulation Agreement (ASSOCIATE IN ENGINEERING)

The Uniform Articulation Agreement promotes educational advancement opportunities for Associate in Engineering (A10500) completers and the constituent institutions of the University of North Carolina in order to complete Bachelor of Science in Engineering degrees. It applies to all N.C. community colleges that operate the A.E. program and to U.N.C. constituent institutions.

The following North Carolina community colleges have received STATE BOARD APPROVAL to offer the Associate in Engineering degree:

Asheville Buncombe Technical Community College

Blue Ridge Community College

Brunswick Community College

Catawba Valley Community College

Central Carolina Community College

Central Piedmont Community College

Coastal Carolina Community College

College of the Albemarle

Craven Community College

Durham Technical Community College

Fayetteville Technical Community College

Forsyth Technical Community College

Gaston College

Guilford Technical Community College

Halifax Community College

Johnston Community College

Mitchell Community College

Nash Community College

Pitt Community College

Richmond Community College

Sandhills Community College

Tri-County Community College

Wake Technical Community College

Wilkes Community College

U.N.C. System ENGINEERING PROGRAMS

East Carolina University

North Carolina Agricultural and Technical University

North Carolina State University

University of North Carolina at Charlotte

Western Carolina University

For the complete Uniform Articulation Agreement (Associate in Engineering) visit:
http://www.nccommunitycolleges.edu; Search: engineering

Uniform Articulation Agreement (R.N. TO B.S.N.)

The Uniform Articulation Agreement promotes educational advancement opportunities for registered nurses moving between North Carolina community colleges and the constituent institutions of the University of North Carolina in order to complete Bachelor of Science in Nursing degrees.

It applies to all N.C. community colleges that operate associate degree nursing programs and to those 11 constituent institutions of the the University of North Carolina that operate R.N. to B.S.N. programs.

NCCCS Associate's Degree NURSING PROGRAMS

Alamance Community College

Asheville-Buncombe Technical Community College

Beaufort County Community College

Bladen Community College

Blue Ridge Community College

Brunswick Community College

Caldwell Community College and Technical Institute

Cape Fear Community College

Carteret Community College

Catawba Valley Community College

Central Carolina Community College

Central Piedmont Community College

Cleveland Community College

Coastal Carolina Community College

College of The Albemarle

Craven Community College

Davidson County Community College

Durham Technical Community College

Edgecombe Community College

Fayetteville Technical Community College

Forsyth Technical Community College

Gaston College

Guilford Technical Community College

Halifax Community College

Haywood Community College

Isothermal Community College

James Sprunt Community College

Johnston Community College

Lenoir Community College

Mayland Community College

McDowell Technical Community College

Mitchell Community College

Nash Community College

Piedmont Community College

Pitt Community College

Randolph Community College

Richmond Community College

Roanoke-Chowan Community College

Robeson Community College

Rockingham Community College

Rowan-Cabarrus Community College

Sampson Community College

Sandhills Community College

South Piedmont Community College

Southeastern Community College

Southwestern Community College

Stanly Community College

Surry Community College

Tri-County Community College

Vance-Granville Community College

Wake Technical Community College

Wayne Community College

Western Piedmont Community College

Wilkes Community College

Wilson Community College

U.N.C. System R.N. TO B.S.N. PROGRAMS

Appalachian State University

Fayetteville State University

East Carolina University

North Carolina Agricultural and Technical University

North Carolina Central University

University of North Carolina at Charlotte

University of North Carolina at Greensboro

University of North Carolina at Pembroke

University of North Carolina at Wilmington

Western Carolina University

Winston-Salem State University

For the complete Uniform Articulation Agreement (R.N. to B.S.N.) visit: http://www.nccommunitycolleges.edu; Search: BSN

INDEPENDENT COMPREHENSIVE Articulation Agreement

The Independent Comprehensive Articulation Agreement (ICAA) between the North Carolina Community College System (NCCCS) and the signatory institutions of North Carolina Independent Colleges and Universities (NCICU) is intended to provide smooth transfer for community college students who wish to continue their education at an NCICU signatory institution. The ultimate goal of this agreement is the seamless articulation from the community college to the NCICU institution with minimal loss of credit or repetition of work.

This ARTICULATION AGREEMENT applies to the following Associate's Degrees:

➔ The Associate in Arts (A10100) (A.A.) degree is designed for students who want to pursue a four-year degree in one of the liberal arts disciplines or training at a professional school that requires a strong liberal arts background.

➔ The Associate in Science (A10400) (A.S.) degree is designed for students who want to pursue a four-year degree in areas of study such as computer science, engineering, mathematics, the sciences or professional programs that require strong mathematics and science backgrounds.

Independent Colleges and Universities that are SIGNATORY INSTITUTIONS of the Independent Comprehensive Articulation Agreement:

Barton College

Belmont Abbey College

Bennett College

Brevard College

Campbell University

Chowan University

Gardner-Webb University

Guilford College

Greensboro College

Lees-McRae College

Lenoir-Rhyne University

Livingstone College

Mars Hill University

Meredith College

Methodist University

Montreat College

North Carolina Wesleyan College

Pfeiffer University

Salem College

Shaw University

St. Andrews College

University of Mount Olive

William Peace University

Wingate University

For Independent Comprehensive Articulation Agreement visit: http://www.nccommunitycolleges.edu; Search: independent CAA

Transfer of Courses Taken in OTHER ASSOCIATE'S DEGREE PROGRAMS

Upon admission to another public two-year institution or to a public university, a community college student who was enrolled in an Associate in Applied Science (A.A.S.) or Associate in Fine Arts (A.F.A.) degree program and who satisfactorily completed the courses with a grade of "C" or better in all courses that are designated for college transfer will receive credit for those courses. A.A.S. or A.F.A. students completing courses designated Universal General Education Transfer Component will receive equivalent general education course credit for those courses at the receiving institution. For courses not designated as Universal General Education Transfer Component, the receiving institution will determine whether the course will count as general education or pre-major/elective credit. Students in these programs who transfer must meet the general education requirements of the receiving institution.

Articulation of Associate in Fine Arts or Associate in Applied Science degree programs may be handled on a bilateral articulation agreement basis rather than on a state-wide basis. Under bilateral agreements, individual universities and one or more community colleges may join in a collaborative effort to facilitate the transfer of students from A.F.A. or A.A.S. degree programs to baccalaureate degree programs.

Transfer of Courses NOT ORIGINATED at North Carolina Community Colleges

Transfer courses that do not originate at a North Carolina community college or U.N.C. institution may be used under the CAA with the following stipulations:

➔ Courses must be completed at a regionally accredited institution of higher education.

➔ Courses must meet general education requirements; and

➔ Courses may total no more than 14 semester hours of general education course credit.

➔ For courses not originating at an N.C. community college, if the courses are used to complete the A.A. or A.S., the courses will transfer as part of the degree. Otherwise, if 14 hours or less are presented without

completion of the A.A. or A.S., then the receiving institution will consider the courses on a course-by-course basis.

For a complete copy of the current Comprehensive Articulation Agreement between The University of North Carolina and The North Carolina Community College System visit: http://www.nccommunitycolleges.edu/ academic-programs/college-transferarticulation-agreements/comprehensive-articulation-agreement-caa

N.C. Comprehensive Articulation Agreement prior to 2014

The original Comprehensive Articulation Agreement was established in 1997. Since then, there have been nearly two decades of student and faculty experience with the CAA, considerable changes in lower-level general education requirements, and major program requirements of our North Carolina public four-year institutions.

Students officially enrolled in an A.A. or A.S. program at a North Carolina community college prior to Fall Semester 2014 are subject to the conditions and protections contained in the CAA in place at the time of their initial enrollment as long as they have remained continuously enrolled. If a student has stopped attending the community college for two or more consecutive terms, they may resume enrollment under the current CAA.

N.C. CAA PRIOR TO 2014

64-65 semester hours of credit for transfer degree

➔ **44 semester hours general education core**

➔ **20 semester hours of additional general education, pre-major and elective courses**

ASSOCIATE IN ARTS	ASSOCIATE IN SCIENCE
ENGLISH - 6 (SHC)	ENGLISH - 6 (SHC)
HUMANITIES & FINE ARTS – 12 (SHC)	HUMANITIES & FINE ARTS – 9 (SHC)
SOCIAL/BEHAVIORAL SCIENCE – 12 (SHC)	SOCIAL/BEHAVIORAL SCIENCE – 9 (SHC)
MATHEMATICS – 6 (SHC)	MATHEMATICS – 6 (SHC)
NATURAL SCIENCE – 8 (SHC)	NATURAL SCIENCE – 8 (SHC)
HEALTH/PHYSICAL ED – 2 (SHC)	ADDITIONAL MATH & SCIENCE – 6 (SHC)
TRANSFER ELECTIVE REQUIREMENTS – 18 (SHC)	HEALTH/PHYSICAL ED/TECHNOLOGY – 2 (SHC)
	TRANSFER ELECTIVE REQUIREMENTS – 20 (SHC)

Transferring to a **NON-PARTICIPATING CAA** University

If you plan to transfer to an out of state university or to a private university in N.C. that does not participate in the CAA, there are important strategies you need to consider to ensure a smooth transfer.

1. **CONTACT THE ADMISSIONS DEPARTMENT** at your prospective university as soon as you determine they are on the list of possible transfer schools. Write down the name of the person you spoke to and send an e-mail follow up after your phone conversations to summarize what you learned.

2. **DISCUSS THE SPECIFIC DEGREE** in which you are enrolled at your community college and whether you plan to complete an associate's degree before transfer, or if you plan to complete a minimum number of credits. Ask about any specific minimum course requirements, including minimum number of credits needed to transfer and specific courses required.

3. **ASK ABOUT THE MAJOR** you plan to pursue at the university and which electives, if any, you can take at the community college.

4. **MANY SCHOOLS HAVE COURSE EQUIVALENCY GUIDES** or websites where you can enter your courses taken and see the equivalent course at the university. This can help you determine the courses for which you may receive credit upon your admission.

5. **ASK ABOUT THE MAXIMUM NUMBER OF CREDITS** you can transfer into the university. Most have a limit on the total number they will accept, either for general education or into your major. Also, you will want to inquire about the minimum grades the new school will accept. For example, many will only take those classes where you earned a "C" or above.

6. **MOST UNIVERSITIES WILL COMPLETE A TRANSFER EVALUATION** upon your acceptance to the school. This will show exactly which classes will transfer.

7. **MOST IMPORTANTLY, STAY IN COMMUNICATION WITH YOUR CONTACT** at the university and ask any questions you have along the way!

Comprehensive Articulation Agreement **TRANSFER CREDIT APPEAL PROCEDURE**

GUIDING PRINCIPLE: If a student from a North Carolina Community College System (NCCCS) college believes the terms of the Comprehensive Articulation Agreement (CAA) have not been honored by a University of North Carolina (U.N.C.) institution to which the student has been admitted, the student may invoke the CAA Transfer Credit Appeal Procedure. Each U.N.C. and community college institution will provide a link to the Transfer Credit Appeal Procedure on its website.

Steps in Filing an **APPEAL**

STEP 1

➜ By the last day of classes of the first semester for which admission is offered, the student must submit a CAA Transfer Credit Appeal Form along with any supporting documentation to the director of admission at the U.N.C. campus to which the student has been admitted. Students first enrolling at the four-year institution in a summer session must submit their appeal by the end of the subsequent fall semester.

➜ The student must specify on the appeal form the specific CAA language that is in contention. Appeals that lack this information will not be considered.

➜ The Director of Admission will review the appeal and respond in writing (email or letter) to the student within 15 business days.

STEP 2

➜ If the student is not satisfied with the decision of the director of admissions, he/she may appeal on the same form to the chief academic officer (provost) of the university within 15 days of written notice of the director's decision.

➜ The provost will review the appeal and respond in writing (email or letter) to the student within 15 business days of receiving the student's appeal.

STEP 3

➜ If the student is not satisfied with the decision of the provost, he/she may appeal to the Transfer Advisory Committee (TAC) subcommittee, composed of the co-chairs, a representative from the U.N.C. General Administration, and a representative from the NCCCS. The student must submit the appeal to the subcommittee within 15 days of the receipt of the provost's decision. The appeal to the TAC subcommittee should be sent to:

> U.N.C.-GA Transfer Advisory Committee Member
> CAA Appeal, PO Box 2688, Chapel Hill, N.C. 27515

If a consensus is reached by the subcommittee, the student will be notified within 15 business days; if a consensus resolution is not reached, the appeal will be forwarded by the subcommittee to the full TAC within 10 business days. The TAC will review the appeal and notify the student of the final decision within 10 business days of receiving the appeal.

Comprehensive Articulation Agreement
TRANSFER CREDIT APPEAL PROCEDURE

University of North Carolina/North Carolina Community College System

SECTION 1: Student Information (to be completed by the student submitting the form)

→ The completed form and any supporting documentation must be submitted to the U.N.C. institution's Director of Admission by the last day of classes of the first semester for which admission is offered.

→ You must specify the nature of the appeal and cite the specific CAA language that is in contention. Appeals that do not include this information cannot be considered.

Last Name: _____ First: _____ MI: _____
(Please print or type)

Address: _____
(Number and Street)   (City)   (State)   (Zip)

Telephone: _____ Email: _____
(Area code/Number)

Last N.C. Community College Attended: _____

U.N.C. institution offering admission: _____ beginning (semester/yr) _____

SECTION 2: Basis for your appeal

→ State your concern(s), citing specific language in the CAA that is applicable to your contention. Attach supporting documents.

→ The CAA may be found at the North Carolina Community Colleges System website: **http://www.nccommunitycolleges.edu/academic-programs/college-transferarticulation-agreements/ comprehensive-articulation-agreement-caa**.

Student Signature: _____ Date: _____

NOTES

Quick **TIPS**

1. Plan early and identify requirements.
Learn the academic requirements for your major early and plan accordingly. Make sure you know if they require prerequisites to be admitted to the program. Also they may have a minimum GPA requirement. Knowing all of this information early can help you be prepared and help with your planning. Some questions you might also want to research are:

→ If you are applying to a closed/competitive program, are you automatically admitted if you meet the minimum requirements for admission?

→ If the requirement is a 2.5 GPA and everyone meets that requirement, how will the admissions team rank the applicants?

2. Know required credentialing.
Know any credential requirements for your field beyond the degree for your major and make them a part of your plan. For example, if you are going to be an accountant, you may need to complete the Certified Public Accountant (CPA) Exam.

3. Talk to people working in the field.
Talk to professionals in your intended career field and find out what they majored in and seek any advice that might better prepare you.

4. Always familiarize yourself with the course catalog.
Know the course descriptions at your community college and your four-year university. Take note of any prerequisites that need to be met.

5. Know your subject strengths.
Are you strong in math and science or writing intensive subjects? Try to match your strengths with subjects required for your major.

6. Balance out your academic schedules.
Spread your difficult subjects evenly throughout your college career to help balance out heavy course loads.

7. Establish a relationship with an admissions counselor.
Getting to know a counselor or professional at the school to which you wish to transfer can go a long way. Some schools even have a name for this: Demonstrated Interest. It means that you have shown someone on their staff that you are truly interested in their university.

8. Know how to calculate your GPA and what it means to be in good academic standing.
For example, in some colleges you must maintain a 2.0 GPA on a 4.0 scale to remain in good academic standing and to keep your financial aid intact. Find out more about these policies at your college. Some questions you might also want to research are:

→ If I make a "D" in a class at my community college is it transferable to the university?

→ If I want a higher grade can retake a class at the community college?

→ If I retake a class, does the previous grade stay on my transcript? What is the procedure to get that higher grade calculated into my GPA?

What if you have a less than ideal **ACADEMIC HISTORY?**

For cases in which a student has a challenging academic history, universities are making strong efforts to help students achieve degree attainment. For example, if the student attended more than one school and there is a significant difference in grades, some colleges will call the student to get more information regarding potential extenuating circumstances. At some colleges, borderline candidates go to a secondary review process. At some universities any GPA below a 2.25 requires review. Sometimes, students with GPAs of 2.0-2.4 will be wait-listed to see if they can pull up their grades in a semester. It is also important to note that, if GPA declines after acceptance, admission to the college can be rescinded.

"We look for *reasons to admit*, not deny."

— JORDAN BULLINGTON, TRANSFER ADMISSIONS COUNSELOR, UNCC

EXERCISE 3.2 | ACADEMIC PROGRAM **EVALUATION**

Now that you have selected your major and minor, you will begin to investigate the academic requirements to graduate with a bachelor's degree in that major. To complete this assignment go to the website of your first choice prospective transfer college/university. Find the program/major that you will pursue and answer the following questions.

Name of University: _____

1. Does this university offer a degree for this major (concentration and/or minor)? List your intended major/program at this university. What is the type of degree (B.A., B.S., etc.)?

2. Where specifically is this major located at the university (department, college of, etc.)?

3. Is this major open or closed? If closed, what are the special academic requirements for admission to the program?

4. What is the total number of credit hours you have to complete in order to graduate with a bachelor's degree in this major from this university?

5. Please save a copy of the academic plan for your major from the university.

Now it's time to figure out what academic requirements you can satisfy while attending the community college, in order to successfully transfer to the university.

6. In which degree should you be enrolled in at the community college in order to transfer to this university for this major?

7. Complete the checklist used at your community college for your associate's degree. If you are only completing the minimum course requirements (MCR), then complete the list of the 24-30 hours you will take. Make sure you look over the program of study for your university and consider what classes you can take at the community college as part of your pre-major requirements that will benefit you the most at the university.

For FIRST YEAR and RETURNING STUDENTS

Log in to your community college transfer website. Select the degree that corresponds with the program in which you are currently enrolled. The checklist will help you identify which classes you need to complete while at the community college in order to satisfy the academic requirements for transfer under the CAA agreement. Complete this assignment by identifying your past, current and future course requirements.

For CAREER and COLLEGE PROMISE STUDENTS

Log in to the Career and College Promise section of your community college website. Select the checklist that corresponds with the program in which you are currently enrolled. The checklist will help you identify which classes you need to complete while at the community college in order to satisfy the academic requirements for transfer under the CAA agreement. Complete this assignment by identifying your past, current and future course requirements.

Suggestions or Instructions for PRE-MAJOR REQUIREMENTS

These courses should be selected based on your intended major (15 SCH).

→ Visit the website for your transfer university.

→ Find your intended major.

→ Review the Academic Plan of Study.

→ Investigate the courses that will fulfill the additional 14 (SHC) of courses that should be selected from courses classified as pre-major, elective or general education courses within the CAA.

For a complete list of transfer courses visit: **http://www.nccommunitycolleges.edu/academic-programs/ college-transferarticulation-agreements/comprehensive-articulation-agreement-caa**

For example: Complete the following eight progression courses at an N.C. community college with a minimum grade of "C" in each course. *From the U.N.C.C. Belk College of Business Transfer Guide.*

N.C. COMMUNITY COLLEGE COURSE	NOTES	✓
ACC 120: Principles of Accounting I		
ACC 121: Principles of Accounting II		
ECO 251: Principles of Microeconomics		
ECO 252: Principles of Macroeconomics		
MAT 263: Brief Calculus or MAT 271: Cal I		
MAT 152: Statistical Analysis		
CIS 110: Introduction to Computers		
BUS 110: Introduction to Business		

Suggestions or Instructions for OTHER REQUIRED HOURS 11-14 additional SCH:

→ These hours are to be taken in addition to the core requirements.

→ Always consult the catalog of the four-year school you plan to transfer to for specific requirements.

→ Consult your community college catalog for a list of all transfer electives available to you.

ACADEMIC PLAN

Semester 1: _____

COURSE REQUIREMENT	CREDITS	GRADE
Total credit hours this semester:		

Semester 2: _____

COURSE REQUIREMENT	CREDITS	GRADE
Total credit hours this semester:		

Semester 3: _____

COURSE REQUIREMENT	CREDITS	GRADE
Total credit hours this semester:		

Semester 4: _____

COURSE REQUIREMENT	CREDITS	GRADE
Total credit hours this semester:		

What is your projected date of completion? _____

NOTES

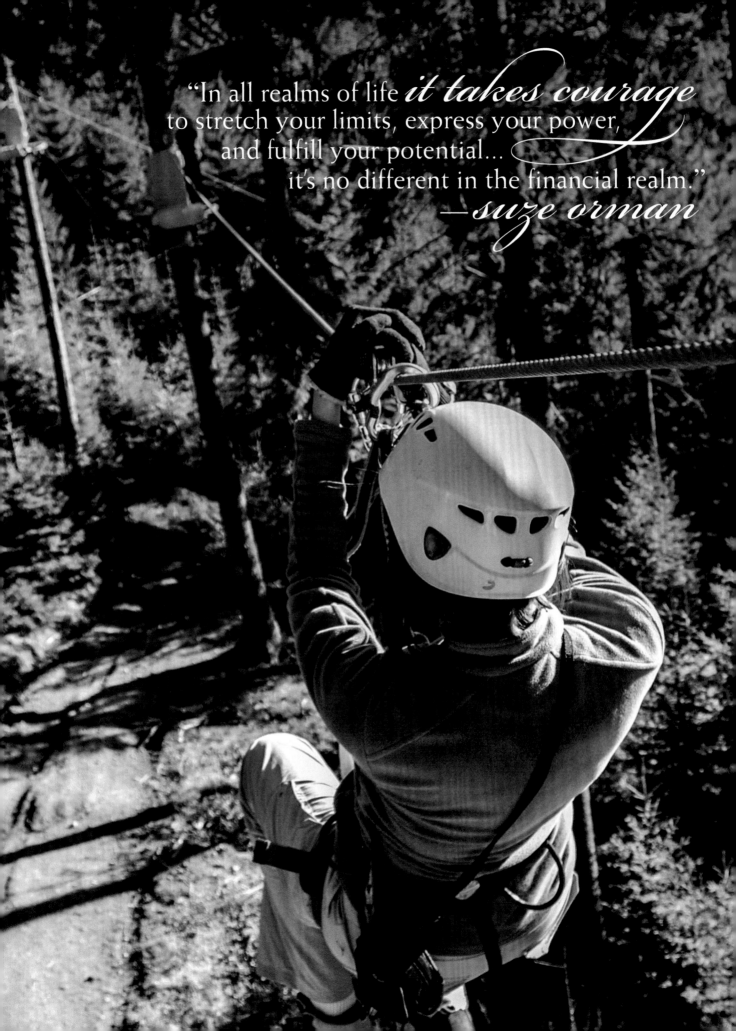

"In all realms of life *it takes courage* to stretch your limits, express your power, and fulfill your potential... it's no different in the financial realm."
—*suze orman*

SECTION 3 | **PAYING FOR COLLEGE**

IN THIS SECTION:

➔ Explore the Cost of College

➔ Investigate Different Sources Available to Pay for College

➔ Research Ways to Save on College Costs

➔ Create a Plan to Pay for College

SECTION 3 | PAYING FOR COLLEGE

Once you have decided on a career and the major that will best prepare you for that career, you will then begin to look at which four-year college or university has the program that fits your needs. In addition to the many other factors you must take into account when choosing the right college, you must also consider the cost. For many, cost is the deciding factor.

In this chapter you will research the total cost of your college expenses, investigate your options for paying, learn about ways to save on costs, and create an overall financial plan to pay for college. According to the College Board, the national average cost for attending college during the 2014-2015 academic year was:

AVERAGE PUBLISHED ANNUAL TUITION & FEES
Two-year public (in-state) $3,347
Four-year public (in-state) $9,139
Four-year public (out-of-state) $22,958
Four-year private $31,231

Associated **EXPENSES**

When you take into account how much you will have to pay to attend college, you have to consider more than the cost of tuition alone. There are many other expenses that contribute to the total cost of your education. The costs associated with college include, but may not be limited to:

TUITION & FEES: Based on number of credit hours the student is taking per semester; may also include other miscellaneous expenses such as lab fees or student activity fees.

ROOM & BOARD: Covers the cost of housing and food plans. The cost varies as some housing on campus may have different cost. The costs will also vary based on whether you live on or off campus.

BOOKS & SUPPLIES: Varies depending on how many classes are taken and the required materials for each. The average yearly cost for books and supplies for a student at a four-year public college was $1,200 in 2014-2015.

PERSONAL EXPENSES: Usually includes cost-of-living, recreation, and personal supplies. The College Board reports that expenses in this category for 2014–2015 ran from $2,609 at private colleges to $3,242 at public universities.

TRANSPORTATION: The cost associated will cover local travel and travel to and from home to campus. Consider the costs of gas, and bus, train or plane fare.

Colleges provide a published price, sometimes called the "sticker price," which includes the cost of tuition and fees, and room and board before factoring in grants, scholarships and financial aid awards. This amount is usually more than the student will actually have to pay. For example, you may be interested in attending a university with a published price of $7,000 per semester. After your financial aid award, the net price may be only $3,150. The "net price" is the total cost of tuition and fees, room and board, and books and supplies after the student has been awarded federal, state and college aid.

Ways to **PAY**

Regardless of the amount you will be expected to pay for your college education, it's imperative that you begin thinking about ways to absorb these costs. Can your family contribute? Have you been saving for college? Do you qualify for federal student aid? Financial aid plays a pivotal role in providing access to college as well as degree completion. It is intended to make up the cost difference between what college costs and what your family can afford to pay. It is based on the premise that all students should have equal access to a college education. Approximately two-thirds of undergraduate students receive some type of financial aid. In 2014, the average amount of financial aid that a full-time undergraduate student received was $14,180.

According to the Department of Education and FAFSA guidelines, students must meet the following eligibility requirements in order to receive federal assistance:

➜ Be enrolled or accepted for enrollment in an eligible program;

➜ Have a high school diploma or GED;

➜ Be a U.S. citizen or eligible non-citizen;

➜ Not be a member of a religious community that directs the program of study or provides maintenance;

➜ Be registered with the Selective Service (males only);

➜ Not be in default on a Title IV student loan borrowed for attendance at any institution;

➜ Not have borrowed in excess of Title IV loan limits;

➜ Not owe a repayment on a Title IV grant or loan received for attendance at any institution;

➜ Maintain satisfactory academic progress;

➜ Not be enrolled concurrently in an elementary or secondary school;

➜ Provide a valid social security number.

If you have been convicted of possessing or selling illegal drugs, you must complete a **DRUG CONVICTION** worksheet to determine eligibility.

TERMS You Should Know

FAFSA (Free Application for Federal Student Aid)
This should be filed as soon after Jan 1st as possible and must be resubmitted each year. Within 4-6 weeks of completion of the FAFSA, the student will receive a document called the Student Aid Report (SAR), which will notify the student if he or she is eligible for the Pell Grant and what the family is expected to contribute to the cost of education.

CSS PROFILE (College Scholarship Service)
A supplemental financial aid application, processed by the College Scholarship Service. Some colleges and universities require the profile to calculate their own institutional financial aid awards.

SAR (Student Aid Report)
Summarizes information included on the FAFSA and reports the expected family contribution (EFC) and eligibility for Pell Grant.

EFC (Expected Family Contribution)
The amount that a student and the student's family are expected to pay toward the student's cost of attendance.

COA (Cost of Attendance)
The total amount of college expenses before financial aid. Cost of attendance includes money spent on tuition and fees, room and board, books and supplies, and living expenses.

NET PRICE CALCULATOR
An online tool that gives you a personalized estimate of what it will cost to attend a specific college. Most colleges are required by law to post a net price calculator on their websites.

Types of FINANCIAL AID

🐷 **GRANTS** are financial aid, based on need, that you do not have to repay. Grants may be given from the federal government, state government, colleges and universities, or public or private institutions.

THE PELL GRANT is the most well-known federal aid grant in the U.S. It began in 1972 and is one of the key areas of funding for low-income students. Eligibility for the Pell Grant is determined by family contribution, full- or part-time status, cost of attendance and length of study. This federal grant ranges from $626 to $5,775 for full-time undergraduate students and is available for a total of 12 full semesters of college attendance.

THE FEDERAL SUPPLEMENTAL EDUCATIONAL OPPORTUNITY GRANT (FSEOG) is another federal grant. This grant is intended to assist students who demonstrate exceptional financial need, with awards ranging from $100 to $4,000 per academic year. Students with a Pell Grant with the lowest EFC are awarded FSEOG awards first. Remaining grants are disbursed to other students until funds are depleted at the college.

There are also grants offered for different categories of students such as race, gender, area of study, and military background. The key is to research all the options and apply early. Many grants have a limited amount of resources and are awarded on a first come, first served basis.

States also offer grants. It is important to research your state to see what grants may be offered. For example, North Carolina offers the N.C. Education Lottery Scholarship Grant. To be eligible, you must:

➔ Be a legal resident of the state of North Carolina.

➔ Be registered as a student with a minimum of 6 credit hours per semester at a college within the state of North Carolina.

➔ Have proof that financial help is needed.

SCHOLARSHIPS are a type of grant used to finance the cost of college. They are usually awarded to undergraduate students and offer awards that don't need to be paid back.

→ Merit-based scholarships are awarded for outstanding academic and/or civic achievements.

→ Need-based scholarships are awarded on the basis of the financial need of the student. These scholarships will require applicants to fill out a Free Application for Federal Student Aid (FAFSA).

→ A combination of merit and need or competitive scholarships can be based on academic excellence, civic achievement, leadership qualities and athletic ability.

General scholarships have a broad nature and can be offered by any individual or organization for various amounts. Scholarships can also be program or major specific. Just remember that there are businesses and organizations in your communities that are interested in recognizing local students by sponsoring scholarships for college. It would be in your best interest to check into local scholarships. An effective search can render scholarships that are specific to a student's skills and interests.

Ways to Find Scholarships

→ **Colleges and Universities** disburse the majority of scholarships available to students. A great place to search is at the four-year colleges that interest you. Also check with the department of your major. There may be scholarships or grants available to students specific to some career fields.

→ **Libraries** have in their holdings numerous books about financial aid and scholarship guides.

→ **Advisors and Counselors** usually maintain a current collection of books and brochures on scholarships and grants. They can also be very helpful with effective application strategies.

→ **Websites** are available to help you find scholarships, grants, and loans that match your skills, interests, talents, and financial background. Be cautious of scholarship sites that offer information for a fee.

→ **Community Organizations and Foundations** often offer scholarships to students for outstanding scholastic achievements, leadership and civic engagement.

→ **Companies/Employers** may offer scholarships or tuition reimbursement (full or partial) to their employees or children of employees.

→ **The Federal Student Aid Information Center** at 1-800-4-FED-AID.

→ **The College/University Financial Aid Office** usually has a list of all scholarships offered to the students attending that institution.

The College Board reports that almost three billion dollars in scholarships is available for college students every year. Many four-year colleges and universities offer scholarships that specifically target transfer students. Make sure you ask about the possibilities when you are researching your prospective four-year colleges.

FEDERAL COLLEGE LOANS are what students and their families depend on more than any other source of financial aid. More than $100 billion in federal education loans and $10 billion in private student loans are originated each year. Educational loans are like other loans—you must repay the money you borrow with interest. However, there are some differences in these loans compared to traditional loans. For example, you do not have to make payments while you are in college and usually start repaying six to nine months after you graduate or stop taking classes. Also, these loans traditionally have lower interest rates and you don't need a credit history to qualify.

There are three general types of loans offered:

1. **Federal Direct Subsidized Stafford Loans**
   These loans are based on financial need. Subsidized means that the government will pay the interest on the loan while the student is in school.

2. **Federal Direct Unsubsidized Stafford Loans**
   Students get Federal Direct Unsubsidized Stafford Loans regardless of need, but will have to pay all interest charges.

3. **Federal Direct PLUS Loans** (Parent Loans for Undergraduate Students)
   Parents of dependent students can take out a Federal Direct PLUS Loan to help pay for their child's education.

Your college education is an investment that will pay off in the long run in terms of a better paying career. In the short term, loans are often a necessary option to help pay for college. The majority of college students will require student loans to help meet their educational expenses, and the average four-year college graduate, student loan debt was $28,950 for 2014. Knowing all of this, it is important to keep in mind that the amount of debt you have upon graduation can have a significant impact on your lifestyle after college. The question of how much to borrow needs to be very carefully considered. According to the Central Piedmont Community College financial aid department, below are some tips for managing your student loan debt.

Managing Student Loan Debt

→ **Do Not Over Borrow!** Borrow only what you need for your current school year educational expenses. If your expenses increase later, you can always request a second loan application up to your maximum eligibility.

→ **Calculate Final Student Loan Debt Total.** Consider how much you will need to borrow to meet all of your educational goals, whether you are pursuing an associate's, bachelor's, master's degree, or beyond.

→ **Consider monthly payment totals.** Calculate what your monthly payments will be on the loan when it comes time to repay the loan. Do you feel this monthly amount will be doable?

→ **Estimate what other expenses you will have after graduation.** What will be the costs of your housing, food, transportation, insurance, credit cards, car payments, etc.?

→ **Consider what the average starting salary is for the career field you plan to enter.** Based on this salary, do you feel comfortable with this loan debt? Also consider what the job outlook is for your career field. Where would be the best place to live upon graduation? Are you willing to move if necessary?

→ **Resist the temptation** to use your student loans for other things beyond your immediate educational expenses.

INSIDE INFORMATION FROM UNIVERSITY ADMISSIONS REPRESENTATIVES

→ Ask how many credits you need to take to keep your financial aid status intact

→ Check the deadlines for university scholarships and FAFSA for each school

→ Use the Net Price Calculator on the university website to help calculate the cost of attendance for you

The Federal **WORK STUDY** Program and **STUDENT EMPLOYMENT**

A great way to help subsidize the cost of college is to obtain employment. There are work programs available that are conducive to a college student's needs. Most any student, regardless of his or her financial status, can find on-campus work that coincides with the student's career goals. Some university programs and departments hire students as lab assistants, researchers and more. Experience working in these areas will increase your knowledge base, expand your network and help you polish your soft skills. The wages for these jobs can be competitive.

🤝 **THE FEDERAL WORK STUDY PROGRAM** is a federally-funded employment program which provides on-campus, part-time employment for students, allowing them to earn a portion of education expenses while attending college. Students must qualify for financial aid in order to be eligible for this program. The colleges/universities are responsible for administering the Federal Work Study Program. Awards vary based on student need and the institution's funding level.

🤝 **STUDENT WORK PROGRAMS** are part-time employment positions available to college students on the university campus. They too offer a competitive wage and are conducive to a college student's needs. Students are not required to be receiving financial aid in order to secure these positions.

🤝 **LEADERSHIP STIPENDS** are sometimes provided to students who hold leadership positions at their respective university/college. Some leadership positions include but are not limited to those in the student government association, residence life/housing, new student orientation and Greek life.

All of these work options on college campuses can contribute to a very rich college experience while helping you gain valuable skills that will transfer into your preferred career after college.

There is also employment available outside of your college campuses but these jobs may not be as flexible with your schedule during academic intense periods such as mid-terms, final exams or when you need to work on a term paper.

What Role Does Your **FAMILY** Play in Paying for College?

The expected family contribution (EFC) is the amount that your family is able to pay toward the cost of your college education. It is usually determined by the federal government or the prospective college. A formula uses the information you report on the FAFSA to analyze and compare your family's financial conditions with other families' financial conditions. This formula calculates the EFC your family can contribute by evaluating your income, assets and family size. The expectation is that a combination of savings, current income and possibly borrowing will help your family meet the EFC. The Financial Aid Office determines your eligibility for financial aid by taking the EFC number to determine a student's financial need.

> ➔ **COA - EFC = Financial Need**
> ➔ **EFC calculation link:** https://bigfuture.collegeboard.org/pay-for-college/paying-your-share/expected-family-contribution-calculator

Considering the family's role in paying for your college education also means having a conversation with your parent(s) or guardian(s) about the cost, what is affordable and who will pay.

A great way to get the dialogue started is to inform your parents that you have decided to go to college and you would like to discuss some of your options with them. Ask for their opinion on your decision to go. This may encourage them to bring up the issue of money themselves.

Here are some talking points for the conversation about money:
- ➜ Can we afford to pay for college?
- ➜ Is there a college fund or savings committed to my education?
- ➜ Can you afford to pay the expected family contribution and how much can you afford to commit yearly?
- ➜ Are you willing to apply for a PLUS loan to help me pay for college?
- ➜ Does your employer offer scholarships for the children of their employees?
- ➜ Can I afford to attend a private college or should I pursue a public education?
- ➜ Can I afford to attend a college out of state?
- ➜ Are you aware of any scholarships from any civic or community organizations that I might qualify for?

What if Your FAMILY CAN'T HELP Pay for College?

Parents undertaking the primary responsibility of paying for their child's education is what federal student aid programs base a student's dependent or independent classification on. If the student is found to be a dependent he or she must report the parents' income on the FAFSA as well.

Independent status is not granted to a student living outside of a parent's home for financial aid purposes. However, there are exceptions which include:

The event in which a student is estranged from a parent(s) due to an extenuating circumstance such physical or emotional abuse, severe estrangement or abandonment, etc.
- ➜ In these cases the student will be able to pursue a "Dependency Override" (an appeal of the dependency status) and will need to provide three letters or documents confirming that validity of the claim. According to the Department of Education and FAFSA guidelines, in order to be declared an independent, the student must provide specified documentation supporting the request for change of status.

You should also be aware that there are conditions that do not warrant independent or self-supporting status. These conditions include if the parent(s):
- ➜ Refuses to contribute to the student's education
- ➜ Refuses to provide required information
- ➜ Lives out-of-state
- ➜ Income is exhausted

Or if the student:
- ➜ Elects not to live with the parents and/or with other relatives
- ➜ Elects not to have communication with the parents
- ➜ Demonstrates total self-sufficiency

One of the strongest financial investments you will make in your lifetime is the cost of your college education. In order to generate the best return on your investment, careful planning is a must. Remember, you must take a good, hard look at the money issues concerning the cost of college.

Ways to **REDUCE COSTS**

1. Attend a community college for your general education requirements.

2. Take the maximum number of courses you can handle each semester and graduate on time.

3. Consider attending a local university and commute from home.

4. Buy used books or shop for reduced prices online.

5. Create a budget for your personal expenses and set spending limits for yourself.

6. Look for campus employment and leadership opportunities that pay stipends and offer tuition reimbursements.

Quick **TIPS**

1. Everyone should fill out the FAFSA. You should submit the FAFSA as soon as possible after January 1. Even if you think you will not qualify for financial aid due to your income, do it anyway. Many scholarships require the FAFSA to be completed as part of the application process as well.

2. Meeting deadlines is paramount. Make sure you meet any deadlines for financial aid, including scholarships and grants. Check with your college to make sure you have exact dates, including any priority deadlines. Those students who meet these deadlines are considered first for financial aid.

3. Know what resources are available to you. If you are not sure at any time, meet with a financial aid advisor at your college. Ask lots of questions. Use www.collegeboard.org and other websites to gather information.

4. Find out exactly how much the college costs that you want to attend. Go to the www.collegeboard.org site and use their college cost calculator. You can total up all your costs and subtract your expected financial aid. This will give you a great target of the actual out-of-pocket costs you can expect.

5. Remember the 12-semester limit for financial aid. Plan your courses and your finances to ensure you have enough financial aid to cover all the semesters you will need to complete your degree.

6. Maintain any required GPA or Satisfactory Academic Progress requirements. Remember that financial aid requires you to maintain certain grade and credit hour requirements to continue. Make sure you ask what these are so you are familiar with the process. Also ask what happens if you withdraw from a class. Does this impact your financial aid? Does your scholarship also require a minimum GPA to continue it year after year?

7. Make sure you know if financial aid covers housing. Can you live off campus and still receive financial aid?

8. Find out what types of payment plans are offered by the school. Some schools require the payment all at once before the semester begins and others will allow payment throughout the semester/year. Research your options.

Note: Major FAFSA Changes Starting in 2017-2018 Academic Year

Recently, President Obama announced two major changes to the FAFSA process. Beginning with the 2017-2018 financial aid application cycle, the FAFSA will be available on October 1 of the year prior to the upcoming award year. Thus, 2017-2018 FAFSA filing will begin on October 1, 2016. By having the FAFSA available earlier, schools and states will be able to provide financial aid information sooner to students and families.

Second, beginning in 2017-2018, FAFSA will collect tax year 2015 income information and not 2016 information. As a result of this change, most students will be able to complete their FAFSAs using information from an already completed tax return. This is in contrast with the current "prior year" process where many applicants submit their FAFSAs before tax returns have been completed, resulting in the need to estimate income and tax information that subsequently needs to be corrected once the tax return is filed; or worse, waiting to complete the FAFSA until after the tax return has been filed.

EXERCISE 3.3A | **FINANCIAL PLAN** FOR COLLEGE

This worksheet will assist you in your financial planning for college. Visit www.collegeboard.org and the website for one of your top college choices to help you complete this worksheet. If you cannot find the answers to the questions on the college website, contact the college directly for an interview with a member of the financial aid staff.

Name of College : _UNCC_

1. What is the priority deadline to apply for financial aid and when are students notified about financial aid award decisions?

March 1st, 2017
- After initial billing is applied to your UNC charlotte student account (3-5 business)

2. How does the financial aid package change from year-to-year (less/more)? What are the academic requirements or other conditions for the renewal of financial aid, including scholarships?

No, apply every year, 2.0 GPA, 66.6% of classes you attempt, complete degree within a max time frame.

3. What happens if your financial aid package is not ready before it's time to register and pay for classes?

You would pay for it and they'll refund you

4. How will you be billed by the college? Will you have to pay the total sum or is there an option to spread the yearly payment out over equal monthly installments?

5. What scholarships does your university offer for transfer students or students in your major or program? How will scholarships be applied to your account?

One of the ways to reduce college cost is to begin your journey at a community college where the cost is typically lower than at four-year colleges/universities. Let's start by looking at the cost you will incur at the community college.

COST INCURRED THIS SEMESTER	
Tuition and fees	
Room/rent	
Board/food	
Books and supplies	
Transportation	
Personal expenses	
Other costs	
TOTAL	

Total up the number of semesters you estimate attending the community college and multiply that by the cost incurred this semester. _____ X _____ = _____

(cost per semester)   (number of semesters)   TOTAL

What is the breakdown of the yearly cost for your first choice transfer university?

—12 credit hours—

YEARLY BREAKDOWN #1 CHOICE	
Tuition and fees	1906.60
Room/rent	
Board/food	10.00
Books and supplies	750.00
Transportation	52.50
Personal expenses	500.00
Other costs	
TOTAL	

—best note

What is the total cost for your transfer university degree? Total up the number of years it will take and multiply that by the cost per year. _____4_____ X _____ = _____

(number of years attending)   (cost per year)   TOTAL

Total cost of community college + total cost of university = cost of undergraduate degree

_____ + _____ = _____

(total cost of community college)   (total cost of university)   (cost of undergraduate degree)

Now that you have a general idea of how much college will cost and the different resources available to help pay for college, what resources do you anticipate using to pay for college?

Applying for financial aid

What other steps do you need to take to ensure funding for your college education?

- maintain a 2.0 GPA
- good attendance

TRANSFER TASK LIST

Create a task list and action plan of the steps you need to take to ensure you meet the goal needed to fund your college education.

ACTIONS	TARGET DATE	NOTES	COMPLETE/ INCOMPLETE
Apply for final aid	Spring 2018		
Apply for degree	go Fall 2018		
Gather documents for aid	Spring 2018		

RESIDENCE HOUSING IN COLLEGE

1. What is the name of the university you are researching for this assignment?

2. Does the university offer residential housing for transfer students?

3. What are the different types of residence halls (dormitories) offered on campus and what are the requirements?

4. What types of meal plans are available and how much do they cost?

5. Are there meal plans available for non-residential/commuter students? If so, at what cost?

6. What is the cost of living on campus? Is on-campus housing covered by financial aid?

7. What is the cost of off-campus housing? Is off-campus housing covered by financial aid?

8. Which is best for your financial needs: living on-campus or off-campus? If on-campus, is there a particular housing area or residence hall you want to apply to (learning communities, fraternity housing, etc.)?

9. What is the application process for on-campus housing and when is the submission deadline?

10. What employment opportunities are available to help subsidize your cost for residence housing?

EXERCISE 3.3C | **SCHOLARSHIP** EXERCISE

List at least one scholarship that you qualify for and would consider applying for under each of these categories. Make sure that you provide a brief description of the scholarship criteria and requirements, the amount and deadlines for each.

COMMUNITY COLLEGE: What scholarships do you qualify for at your community college?

COMMUNITY COLLEGE SCHOLARSHIPS	
Description	
Academic requirements	
Need- or merit-based	
Amount of award	
Deadline	

UNIVERSITY OR MAJOR/PROGRAM: What scholarships are available based on your area of interest or program/major?

PROGRAM/MAJOR SCHOLARSHIPS	
Description	
Academic requirements	
Need- or merit-based	
Amount of award	
Deadline	

COMMUNITY: What scholarships are available to you in your community or through your employer that you qualify and plan to apply for?

COMMUNITY/EMPLOYER SCHOLARSHIPS	
Description	
Academic requirements	
Need- or merit-based	
Amount of award	
Deadline	

NOTES

MAKING THE
TRANSITION

4

→ Transitioning Successfully

"Give a man a fish and you feed him for a day.
teach a man to fish and
you feed him for a lifetime."
—chinese proverb

MAKING THE TRANSITION

IN THIS SECTION:

→ Making the Final Decision

→ Transitioning Successfully

→ How Universities Help Ensure Your Successful Transition

→ Final Words of Wisdom

MAKING THE TRANSITION

Congratulations! You have researched and planned and are now ready to make your final decision on where you will continue your education. Let's take a moment to revisit the Five Phases of College Transfer Success.

Phase 1: You have oriented yourself to college life, learned about personal responsibility, familiarized yourself with navigating college systems, and explored learning strategies.

Phase 2: You have assessed yourself, chosen your career and major, and begun to establish career and academic goals.

Phase 3: You have researched different college cultures, identified your individual college needs, identified the best colleges for your career choice and major, and re-

searched the cost of attending college. You have also evaluated specific academic degree requirements, reviewed the requirements of the Comprehensive Articulation Agreements and created an academic plan for transfer.

Phase 4: You have explored the college admissions requirements, conducted informational interviews with your top college choices, created an admissions tracking system and completed your transfer and financial aid applications.

Phase 5: Lastly, you will evaluate your transfer college options, make a decision on which will be your best fit, prepare for a successful transition to your transfer college/university and identify resources conducive to a successful transfer transition.

Be Your Own BEST ADVOCATE

"As a student preparing to transfer, this can be as simple as asking any and all questions you may have. Yes, you know how to be a student, but you will need to learn a new campus culture. Don't be afraid to ask questions throughout the transfer process—while completing the application, attending orientation and in your first several weeks and months at your new institution. More than likely the resources are available (and free!), but the office that provides them may have a different name than your former institution. We ultimately want you to succeed and love your college experience but we can only do and anticipate so much for you. *Be your own best advocate* to make the most of your college experience!"

— ERICA ANGALAY, ASSOCIATE DIRECTOR, TRANSFER & NON-TRADITIONAL ADMISSIONS
UNIVERSITY OF NORTH CAROLINA WILMINGTON

Making the **FINAL DECISION**

If you have been accepted to more than one college, you will be faced with the big decision of which is the best college for you. To help you with this, evaluate the following factors:

→ How do you feel about the college in general?

→ Has anything changed in your personal situation since you applied that may influence the choice of one school over another?

→ Is this the right college culture?

→ What's the size of the student body? Is the campus size ideal?

→ Did you get accepted into your major?

→ How large or small are the classes?

→ How many of your community college credits will this college accept?

→ When will you be able to graduate?

→ Did you visit the campus? How was it?

→ How much in financial aid and scholarships will you get?

→ How much out-of-pocket cost is involved?

→ What is the housing situation? Will it fit your needs?

COMMITMENT and Next Steps

You have now made your final decision on where you will complete your education. Here is a list of items you should be sure to complete once you have decided which university you will attend. Later in this unit you will have the opportunity to create a "Task List" and may want to include these items, along with specific dates in your action plan.

→ Use the formal process of accepting admission to notify the university in writing that you have decided to attend.

→ Contact admissions and/or the college business office to find out when tuition and fees are due and how they must be paid. Confirm your financial aid in your university account.

→ Contact campus housing to reserve your space with a deposit and find out when move-in is allowed.

→ Sign up for new and/or transfer student orientation.

→ Contact your new faculty advisor for your major to schedule your first official advising session. Note: signing up for classes is often part of orientation, so ask if it will be part of this process or if you need to meet with an advisor prior to orientation.

→ Complete and submit any health history and/or immunization forms.

→ When you meet with your academic advisor at your four-year school, make sure to review your degree evaluation to understand what courses have transferred from your community college to the university. You need to have a clear understanding of exactly how many college credits are remaining to graduate. If a community college course has not been transferred to a four-year school the way you thought it would be, discuss this with the academic advisor. It is important to have the syllabus and course description from the semester in which you took the course at the community college when you have this discussion. You might be surprised at how far a well-researched justification can get you.

→ Have an official copy of your final transcript sent to the university.

Remember to follow through with maintaining your strong academic record until you leave the community college, even after being accepted to the university. Your admission decision can be rescinded if your grades fall below the required GPA or you have any academic or disciplinary violations.

Transitioning SUCCESSFULLY

You are ready to go. Let's take a minute to think about the actual transition you are about to make and honor some of the things you may be feeling about this upcoming change in your life.

You have made other changes in your life up to this point. There are two parts of change: the actual event, such as getting married, losing someone, getting a new job, losing a job, going to college for the first time, transferring to a new college, moving, graduating high school, etc., and the transition, which is the psychological/emotional side of the process. It is important to think about both of these parts of the change.

We usually think more about the actual "event" and create a to-do list of the things we need to make this happen. For example, if you are moving, you plan the move date, get people to help you move your belongings, find boxes and packing materials, call the cable and power companies to turn off and turn on your utilities, etc. But sometimes you do not take the time to think about the personal impact moving may have on your day-to-day life.

Think back about changes or transitions you have made in your life. When you are getting ready to make a change in your life, what are some of the things you need to do for yourself from a personal and emotional standpoint? Some of the most helpful things are to remember your goals and what your purpose is—your mission. Remember how to advocate for yourself and make sure to give yourself time to get comfortable with the new reality. Take some time to also think about the personal impact of the change and make a plan of how you will help yourself move through this transition as well as who can support you in this process.

WORRIED ABOUT CHANGE?

Sometimes we get fearful or worried about change. Here are questions you can ask yourself during these times.

QUESTIONS TO ANSWER

→ What can you do something about? Are you willing to do it? Who can help you?

→ What do you have to accept? Are you willing to accept this? Who can help you?

Asking yourself these questions gives you the power and confidence to take action in one form or another.

One tool that can also assist you as you think about this transition is a model developed by William Bridges in 1991 called the **Transitions Model**. Bridges says that during times of transition we go through specific steps and have particular feelings as we move along. He breaks this process down into three stages:

1. **Endings**

2. **Neutral Zone**

3. **New Beginnings**

The **TRANSITIONS MODEL**

STAGE 1 Endings

This is the initial stage of transition. You will be moving away from what has been familiar and comfortable. You are accustomed to your current college campus and know where all of the classrooms and offices are located. You have built relationships with instructors, college professionals and fellow students. The prospect of letting go of this environment might be met with some resistance.

During the "Endings" stage, you may feel:

1. **Fear, denial or anger**
2. **Sadness or disorientation**
3. **Frustration or uncertainty**

Things you can do to help ease the transition are:

→ **Communicate what you are feeling**

→ **Be proud of your accomplishments and embrace the change**

→ **Establish support with other students who are experiencing this stage**

→ **Identify and utilize the resources available to help you succeed in the new environment, such as visiting the Transfer Resource Center at your college and attending a transfer student orientation**

→ **Polish up your knowledge and skills by taking advantage of training or learning opportunities**

STAGE 2 Neutral Zone

This stage is more like the bridge from the old to the new. Students are still attached to the old college environment while trying to adapt to the new college environment. An example of this phase might be a student taking final exams and getting ready for graduation from community college, while registering for the right courses to take during his or her first semester, and while finding a place to live at the new university. Managing the change is imperative at this stage, as you are learning the new polices and processes at the new university. You should expect some uncertainty and confusion. But you should also remember that there are trained professionals there to answer your questions.

During the "Neutral Zone" stage you may experience:

1. **Low morale and low productivity**
2. **Anxiety about your role, status or identity at the new school**
3. **Skepticism about how you will fit in and be successful in your new environment**

Things you can do to help ease this transition are:

→ **Meet with your new advisors to confirm you are on track**

→ **Establish your personal and academic goals for the upcoming semester**

→ **Start building relationships with fellow students and peer advisors**

→ **Attend campus programs/events and begin carving out your place on the campus**

→ **Attend a "time management" workshop to help find balance**

STAGE 3 New Beginnings

In this last stage you will experience acceptance and new-found energy. You will begin to feel a sense of accomplishment and see the reward for your hard work. This is where you will begin to embrace the change. As you begin to experience the energy and motivation related to the adoption of the change, you must also find ways to sustain it.

During the "New Beginnings" stage, you may feel:

1. **High energy**
2. **Openness to learning**
3. **Renewed commitment to your goals**

Things you can do to sustain your momentum are:

→ **Keep your personal and academic goals visible**

→ **Stay organized**

→ **Continue cultivating the new relationships you have formed**

→ **Celebrate your small wins and reward yourself for your hard work**

→ **Attend student success programs/workshops**

→ **Join a new club or organization and get involved on campus**

Remember that everyone goes through the phases at their own pace. You may move quickly or sometimes feel stuck. This road may be bumpy at times and you may even make some mistakes along the way. Change can be difficult. It requires self-motivation and a strong commitment to your success.

How Universities HELP ENSURE Your SUCCESSFUL TRANSITION

The great news is your university has created programs and support tools for you as you make your transition. Here are some examples of how they want to help you achieve success on your new college campus:

→ Guided tours for transfer students by transfer students

→ Mentorship programs that connect you at the beginning

→ Courses or workshops about transitioning to the university, graduation and beyond

→ Transfer ambassadors who serve incoming transfers

→ Social activities targeted to transfer students

→ Transfer student associations and honor societies

Other things you may want to consider to help you get acclimated more quickly and to find your place on your new campus include:

→ Getting a job on campus   → Joining a club or organization   → Living on campus the first year

→ Talking to other students in class, reaching out   → Seeking out transfer organizations and groups

The bottom line is you need to seek out events and organizations that are dedicated to transfer student success. Universities have numerous people and processes in place to help you find your way and feel at home at your new college.

"The thing that helped me the most in my transition from a community college to my university was *knowing the right questions* to ask. I met with an advisor at CPCC and at the university and made sure that I was on the right track for both schools. In my first semester at my university, I attended a transfer student seminar with my transfer advisor and I was taught things I never knew I didn't know! I was told how to continue in my university education and the benefits that my university provided me. I also got involved in a few different professional organizations on campus. Being involved in those organizations gave me different resources in terms of staff members at my university and other students who were more experienced than I was in a university experience. From there, I made sure to keep myself surrounded with people who supported and helped my transition from a community college to my university."

— RILEY ANN DEMOCKO,
THE UNIVERSITY OF NORTH
CAROLINA AT CHARLOTTE

Always Have a **PLAN B**

Sometimes despite your best efforts, things don't work out as you planned. In such cases, everyone should have a "Plan B." Plan B is a popular term used to mean a reserved, secondary plan, in case a first plan (a hypothetical "Plan A") fails. This is similar to your parallel plan mentioned in the career discussion in Unit 2, Section 3.

To create your Plan B, choose and apply to more than just your top transfer college choice. Have at least two or three fall-back options in case you do not get into your first-choice school. Sometimes if you don't get in on your first try, you can take courses at another college to demonstrate you can handle the workload if you decide to reapply to your first-choice school.

It is possible you may get to your four-year university and things may not work out as planned. Maybe you have issues with your finances, family obligations or other life events that prevent you from completing your education at that school. Make sure before you choose to leave that you exhaust every effort to make it work. Try using some of the student support services available to you at the university. For academic issues, meet with your professor and look into tutoring. For financial issues you may want to look into part-time work or unclaimed scholarships. If you have trouble with your roommate or living in the residence halls, the housing office can help you resolve roommate conflicts or secure other housing arrangements. If none of these resolve your issue and you find that it is best to leave, don't feel like a failure.

Take whatever steps you need to exit that institution with dignity and go to your Plan B scenario. Take care to ensure you have withdrawn from your courses if necessary and have spoken to your advisors and counselors. You will want to make sure you leave in good standing and that such good standing is reflected on your academic record. You can then take your experiences, learn from those and move to your Plan B as soon as you are able. Also, find out if you are eligible for a refund of your tuition and fees. The money can help you get started on Plan B.

Final **THOUGHTS**

Our journey to transferring successfully has come to an end. But in reality this is just the beginning: the beginning of a new chapter in your life, your mission and your educational journey. We hope the information and techniques learned in this course will provide you with the knowledge and confidence needed to successfully transition into a university environment. Additionally, we hope this transition will help bring to fruition your goals of graduating with a bachelor's degree, your successful entry into the career of your choosing and living your best life. While you will have many people you can go to for advice, such as advisors, counselors, friends and family, we hope you will realize you have the power to create the kind of future you want.

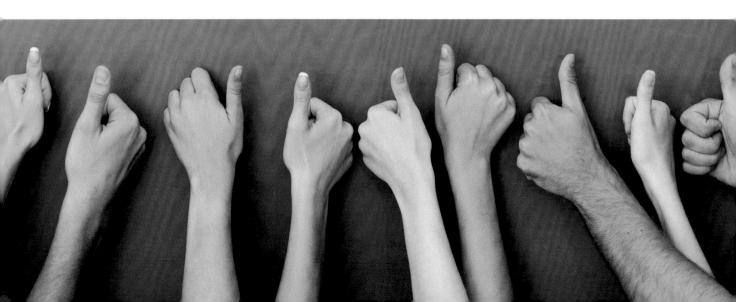

Final WORDS OF WISDOM from Transfer Students

"I wish that I could have worked even more closely with professors to make a name for myself in some of my first courses. I would also suggest that one make the effort to pay close attention to the advice of the professors when they make small hints for assignments and provide suggestions. I think that when students have questions, they should act accordingly to find resources that will assist in a solution. I would like to say finally that I wish I had made attempts in finding these solutions sooner than I did."

— ALLEN LEE DOWLER JR., UNCW TRANSFER STUDENT FROM COASTAL CAROLINA COMMUNITY COLLEGE

"I wish I had spent more time learning about my transition before it happened. Even though I met with advisors to make sure I was all set in terms of the classes and requirements I was engaging in, I wish I had spent more time reaching out to other transfer students to see what experiences they've had in their transition. Getting feedback from other transfer students would have helped me frame a mindset for what my experience would have been. I would strongly advise any transfer student to network as much as you can. Reach out to as many people as you can, regardless of whether it's an advisor, transfer student at your desired university, any other transfer student, family, friends, etc. There are so many people out there who are available to help you throughout this entire process that it makes no sense for any transfer student to be left without answers to their questions!"

— RILEY ANN DEMOCKO, UNCC TRANSFER STUDENT FROM CENTRAL PIEDMONT COMMUNITY COLLEGE

"What helped me most in my transition from the military to the university was recognizing when I needed help and looking to my instructors for it. If you are struggling, recognize that and reach out for help. My instructors were able to guide me on how best to study for their exams, manage my time and point me to the resources available on campus to help me. Be honest with yourself, know yourself and seek self-improvement. The student-teacher relationship has nothing to do with how many students are in the class; it has everything to do with you and the effort you put into building that relationship. Make an effort to connect with a few students in each class and create study groups."

— PATTY MARTINEZ, UNCW TRANSFER STUDENT FROM THE UNITED STATES MARINE CORPS

"My first semester entering the university I learned to be proactive and prepared before meeting with college representatives about my schedule and academic goals. My knowledge of processes and focus on utilizing a monthly planner gave me the confidence needed to incorporate each step of the strategic plan for transferring that I learned at CPCC in the ACA 122 course. This simple process made achieving academic success a fun experience. I graduated from the university at the top of my class and am currently a graduate school student pursuing a master's degree in public history. I would like to share with future students that there are so many resources at the community college and the university to help you, especially when you are finding it difficult. Find them and use them."

— THOMAS TILLMAN, UNCC TRANSFER STUDENT FROM CENTRAL PIEDMONT COMMUNITY COLLEGE

"My first semester I was able to learn more about different clubs and Greek life to find out what best fit my interests. I also joined a learning community, which I would highly recommend. It put me in a group of people who were all transfer students but also in the same major, so we have the same interests and can talk about our experiences with transferring.

- Do your best, nobody wants you to fail. And there will almost always be somebody willing to help; all you have to do is ask.
- Don't be dismayed if you fail a paper or test or even a class. It will be okay; life happens to the best of us. Learn from your mistakes and remember: sometimes you have to make them a few times before you get the hang of it.
- Show up for class. It may sound cliché, but I promise that it will have a positive impact on your grade.
- Don't give up. There will hard days, but other days you will feel like a rock star. Live for those days and learn from the hard days."

— McKENNA SMITH, UNCC TRANSFER STUDENT FROM CENTRAL PIEDMONT COMMUNITY COLLEGE

EXERCISE 4.1 | MAKING THE **TRANSITION REFLECTION** & **TRANSFER ACTION** PLAN

You made it! Take some time now to reflect on your decision and create a "Task List" of the next steps for your transfer plan.

1. On a scale of 1-10 (1 is low and 10 is high), how confident are you at this time with your transfer plans? Explain where you are and how you are feeling at this point.

2. What do you still need more information about to complete your transfer plan?

3. What are three things you can do once you are at your university to ensure your successful degree completion? Note: Making it to the university is one of your first goals. Acclimating to the new university and graduating from there with your bachelor's degree is the second goal!

Now take some time to create a list of the next 4-5 tasks you need to complete as you begin your transfer process. There are some ideas listed below to get you started.

TRANSFER ACTION PLAN

	TASK	NOTES	TARGET DATE	STATUS
Sample 1	Meet with my advisor to ensure I have solid plans for the rest of my classes at the community college and a time-line for transfer.	Bring a copy of the program of study for biology at ECU to this meeting.	December 2017	
Sample 2	Transfer to ECU and major in Biology.		Fall 2018	
Sample 3	Attend Transfer Student Orientation.	Schedule will be posted on ECU website. There is also a special orientation program for transfer students.	Summer 2018	
Task 1				
Task 2				
Task 3				
Task 4				
Task 5				

APPENDIX | COLLEGE ROAD MAP

As you think about the next two to four years, the following checklist will prove helpful to you in terms of planning the key activities you may want to do each year to prepare for your life after college. This document is designed to work as a guide toward your college success. Feel free to add additional items that may pertain to your individual collegiate journey.

FIRST YEAR (College Freshman): Acclimating Yourself to College Life

→ Set goals for the year.

→ Get to know yourself and how you fit into college life.

→ Explore your academic and extracurricular interests.

→ Locate and visit important campus resources and offices (financial aid, student life, academic/tutoring services, registration, disability services, campus security, computer lab, health center).

→ Adjust to your new environment and the freedom/responsibility that go along with it.

→ Assess your study skills and habits; improve them if they need work.

→ Figure out the difference in the academic demands from your previous school and find resources that will contribute to your success.

→ Explore clubs and organizations that interest you.

→ Talk to other students for advice about their majors, classes and professors.

→ Start to become aware of people in roles who are doing work that is interesting to you.

→ Consider a job, an internship or a volunteer experience in an area that interests you.

→ Begin researching career and major possibilities.

→ Meet with your academic advisor to explore requirements for transfer to a university and your course schedule for next semester.

→ Enroll in a transfer degree program.

→ Begin researching prospective four-year colleges and admissions information.

SECOND YEAR (College Sophomore): Exploring Careers and Majors

→ Set goals for the year.

→ Meet with your faculty advisor to discuss majors and course planning options. Establish your academic plan.

→ Establish a strong relationship with career services and find out what insights they provide on career direction. Map out your career plan. Conduct a more detailed exploration of occupations and possibilities. Identify possible career field options.

→ Learn how to network and cultivate mentors. Start attending networking events. Create a tracking system for your contacts. Attend career fairs and workshops and start making contacts.

→ Conduct informational interviews with people working in career fields that interest you.

→ Get more invested in leadership opportunities and extracurricular activities. Find out what organizations related to your career or major exist. Consider running for an executive position within an organization.

→ Start exploring service learning and volunteer opportunities. Get hands-on experience by using your breaks and vacations to volunteer and intern.

→ Select your major and concentration or minor.

→ Keep a journal of your experiences and the skills you are gaining while in college.

→ Begin looking into graduate schools and requirements (exams, GPA requirements, costs, fellowships, etc.).

- → Decide on the transfer colleges you will apply to.
- → Meet with your faculty advisor to make sure you are on schedule to graduate and transfer.
- → Conduct campus visits for top college transfer choices.
- → Plan living arrangements for next year.
- → Apply for graduation at your community college.

THIRD YEAR (College Junior): Building Your Marketing Plan

- → Set goals for career-related interning, volunteering, and summer job experience.
- → Everything that you do should be geared toward the career path you've chosen.
- → Talk to prospective employers about possible jobs and internships and be willing to accept non-paying positions.
- → Prioritize your interests and begin creating your career marketing plan. Build a portfolio.
- → Choose academic electives that enhance your learning and career goals.
- → Get a head start on preparing for grad school admissions processes. Take any grad school exams (LSAT, MCAT, GRE, etc.). This will allow time to retake them if needed.
- → Conduct career research. Target and research potential employers or companies and areas in which you wish to pursue your career.
- → Hone your job search skills and techniques (communication, interpersonal, research, networking, interviewing). Start working closely with career services to create a solid resume and get it out there. Practice and improve your interviewing skills. Start working on your interview attire. Update resume to reflect current experiences.
- → Increase your networking skills.
- → Start connecting with alumni in your field of interest.
- → Reassess your extracurricular activities. Look for more challenging opportunities.
- → Continually refine your job search or graduate school plans.
- → Plan your senior year and create a to-do checklist. This will help to minimize possible stress during your senior year.

FOURTH YEAR (College Senior): Transitioning to Life After College

- → Meet with your advisor to make sure that you're on track to graduate this year.
- → Apply for graduation.
- → Network and make the most of your college's career fairs, forums, and employment readiness workshops. Consider volunteering for some of the events to get the inside track.
- → Research potential employers. Identify relevant periodicals and trade journals. Bone up on new trends in your specialty area. Develop a job search strategy.
- → Visit career services. Brush up on your interviewing skills and refine your resume.
- → Polish up your interviewing attire.
- → Clean up your online image. Make sure you Google yourself and check your Facebook, Twitter and other online profiles.
- → Apply to graduate school if you're planning to go.
- → Make contact with your references, get their permission to use their names and obtain the correct contact information for them.
- → Plan to make your transition to life after college. Where will you live? How will you get to work? What if the job you really want doesn't work out? What is your back-up plan?
- → Take your finals and graduate!

INDEX

Academic advising, 37, 40

Academic course requirements, 131

Academic dishonesty, 23–24

Academic integrity, 3, 9, 23–24

Academic learning center, 37, 40

Academic plan, 4, 37, 144–146, 168, 178

Academic probation, 25

Academic status, 27

Academic suspension, 25

Academic warning, 25

Accountability, 11–12, 71

Admissions, 1, 3–4, 25, 40, 63, 90, 105, 107, 109, 111–117, 120–125, 129, 133–134, 139–140, 143, 154, 168–169, 178–179

Admissions essays, 116

Andragogy, 44–45, 109–110

AngaLay, Erica, 168

Artistic (Creators), 72

Associate's Degree Nursing (ADN), 136

Associate in Arts (AA), 95, 131–135, 137, 139

Associate in Engineering (AE), 135

Associate in Science (AS), 131–135, 137, 139

Basic skills survey, 76

Bass, James, 85

"Begin with the End in Mind," 93

Bridges, William, 170

Briggs Myers, Isabel, 74

Brown, Marquis, 59

Building your network and professional brand, 99

Bullington, Jordan 143

CAA curriculum, 135, 139

Campus housing, 19, 113, 123–124, 169

Campus life, 112, 114, 118, 120–121

Campus size, 112, 119, 169

CareerBuilder, 99

Career counselors, 83

Career development program, 68

Career exploration, 2–3, 67, 79, 87, 91

Career research, 79–81, 83, 88–89, 96, 100, 179

Career services, 2, 40, 73, 83, 88, 99, 113–114, 178–179

Certification, 98, 129

CFNC, 70, 74, 76, 133–134

Changing job market, 95

Cheating, 24
   consequences, 24

Choosing career and major
   assessing yourself, 68
   researching, 2–4, 65, 68, 79–80, 89, 95, 100, 120, 129, 153, 161, 178
   evaluating options, 3–4, 21, 24, 65, 68, 79–80, 89, 119, 131, 155
   making a decision, 68
   implementation, 21, 65, 91, 93, 132

Closed or competitive major, 130

College account, 30

College application, 20, 44, 90, 113–117, 121–124, 133, 151, 153–154, 157, 161, 168

College Board, 118, 153, 155, 157–158

College catalog, 30, 37, 129–130, 145

College culture, 2, 4, 37, 105, 107, 109, 118, 120, 125, 169

College major, 90

College major myths, 87–88

College Scholarship Service Profile (CSS Profile), 151

College visit checklist, 112

Common App, 115, 121

Components of an online portfolio, 98

Comprehensive Articulation Agreements, 4, 105, 127–128, 132, 168

Constituent institutions of the University of North Carolina system, 132–133, 135–136

Conventional (Organizers), 72

Cooperative education, 85

Cost of college, 149, 153, 155–156

Counseling services, 3, 37, 40

Course description, 30–31, 130, 169

Course planning, 2, 4, 105, 127–128, 178

Covey, Stephen, 93

Critical thinking, 2, 9, 18–22, 39, 88, 101

Critical thinking map, 19, 21–22

Culture of adult learning, 44

Daily task list, 15–16, 125, 160, 169, 176

Decision making styles, 20

Democko, Riley Ann, 173, 175

Disability services, 37, 178

"Do What You Are," 74

Dowler, Lee, 175

Elective courses, 89, 95, 130, 133–134, 138

Emotional intelligence, 11

Enterprising (Persuaders), 72

Expected Family Contribution (EFC), 151, 155

Faculty/student support, 23, 38–39, 98, 112–114, 118–119, 121, 134, 138, 169, 178–179

Federal college loans, 154

Federal work study, 155

Final words of wisdom from transfer students, 175

Financial aid, 2–5, 25, 30, 40, 111–114, 117, 121, 123–124, 143, 150–158, 161, 168–169, 178

Free Application for Federal Student Aid (FAFSA), 153

General education courses, 129–130, 133–134, 145

Goal setting, 93–94
    5 Rules of, 94

Grade Point Average (GPA), 25, 30, 89, 132

Grants, 98, 150, 152–153, 157

Holland Codes, 72–73

Holland, John, 72–73

Housman, Donna, ii, iii

Independent Comprehensive Articulation
    Agreement, 137

Industry associations, 99

Industry-specific blogs, 99

Information interview, 79, 83–84, 113

Interdependence, 11

Interest profiler, 73–74

Internships, 39, 84–85, 89, 98–99, 112, 114, 119, 179

Investigative (Thinkers), 72

Kohl, Dave, 94

Leadership stipends, 155

Learning Management System (LMS) (Blackboard, Moodle), 31, 33, 36

Learning strategies, 3, 7, 10, 30, 37, 43–44, 47–48, 63, 168

Learning styles, 43, 47, 49

Letters of recommendation, 98, 113, 115

Library services, 3, 38

Lindeman, E.C., 44

LinkedIN, 95, 97, 99

Loans, 153–154

Lore, Nicholas (The Pathfinder), 74

Lowry, Don, 74

Major concentration, 130

Majors, 68, 72–73, 87–89, 96, 101, 110, 112, 114, 129–131, 133–134, 178

Make your degree marketable, 95

Making the transition to your transfer university, 134

Managing student loan debt, 154

Martinez, Patty, 175

Memory, 46, 48, 53–55, 63

Minimum Course Requirements (MCR), 134, 144

Minor, 50, 56, 84, 89–90, 123–124, 130, 144, 178

Mnemonics, 54

Myers-Briggs Type Indicator (MBTI), 74

Netiquette, 33

Net Price Calculator, 151, 154

Networking, 85, 95–97, 99, 109, 178–179

Note taking, 51, 56–61, 63
    Cornell note taking system, 57–58
    Mind mapping, 56
    Standard outline, 56
    Symbols and abbreviations, 60

Occupational Outlook Handbook, 80–81

O*NET, 73, 76–77, 80–81

Online image, 96–97, 179

Online learning, 29, 32–34, 36, 44

Online professional profile, 96

Open major, 130

Organizing your admissions process, 107, 112, 114, 116

Out of state transfer, 118, 134, 150, 156

Parallel plan, 87, 89–90, 100, 174

Part-time and full-time course load, 130

Paying for college, 2, 105, 149–150, 155
    Annual tuition and fees, 3, 19, 110, 117, 150–151, 153, 157, 159, 169, 174
    Associated expenses, 150
    Ways to pay, 151
    Ways to reduce costs, 157

Pedagogy, 44–45, 109

Personality assessments, 74

personalitypage, 75

Personality type, 74–75

Personal responsibility, 3, 9–12, 30, 33, 44, 62, 168

Phases of college transfer success, 3, 168

Plagiarism, 3, 24

Plan B, 174

Pre-major courses, 133–134

Pre-professional programs, 130

Processing information, 46

Professional brand, 91, 99

Program of study, 30, 90, 109, 144, 151, 177

Purdue University, 73

References, 98, 113–115, 122–124, 179

Registration, 3, 30, 38, 113–114, 178

Residence life, 38, 40, 155

Resume, 138, 179

Right livelihood, 74

Satisfactory Academic Progress, 3, 151, 157

Scholarships, 2, 24, 98, 111, 113–114, 117, 121, 150, 153–154, 156–158, 162, 169, 174

Self-analysis, 14

Self-assessment, 3, 68, 80, 89

Self-awareness, 11, 68, 75

Self-discovery, 3, 68

Self-efficacy, 11

Self-motivation, 11, 172

Semester Hours Credit (SHC), 134

Service learning, 39, 76, 85, 178

Seven Habits of Highly Effective People, 93

Sexual assault/harassment, 25

Short-term goal, 95

Situational reactions, 12

Skills, 2–3, 5, 11, 18, 32–37, 39–40, 46, 49, 51–52, 60–61, 63, 67–68, 76–77, 80–85, 88, 90, 95–101, 114, 116, 134, 153, 155, 171, 178–179

SMART goals, 94

Smith, McKenna, 111, 175

Social (Helpers), 72

Strong Interest Inventory, 74

Student affairs, 2, 37–38, 129

Student aid Report (SAR), 151

Student Code of Conduct, 9, 23

Student handbook, 23

Student leadership, 29, 39, 85, 93

Student success, 3, 13, 32, 37, 49, 85, 93, 109, 172

Student work programs, 117, 155

Study strategies, 49–50

Sutkowski, Owen, 2

Syllabus, 15, 31, 51, 169

Tarrano, Alana, 5

Terminal degree, 130–131

Test taking skills, 63

Tillman, Thomas, 175

Time management and prioritizing, 12

Title IX, 25

Transcripts, 30, 38, 98, 113–115, 122–124

Transferable courses, 130

Transferable skills, 76

Transferable skills checklist, 76

Transfer Articulation Agreements, 4, 127

Transfer Assured Admissions Policy (TAAP), 3, 133

Transfer credit appeal procedure, 139, 141

Transfer degree majors, 131

True colors, 74

Types of financial aid, 152

Uniform Articulation Agreements, 135–137

Universal General Education Transfer Component (UGETC), 3, 134

University of Missouri career services, 73

University of North Carolina system, constituent institutions of the, 132–133, 135–136

Values, 24, 67–71, 80, 82, 89–91, 93–95, 100, 109

Volunteering, 76, 179

"What can I do with this major?" 90

Williams, Alyssa, ii, iii

Work content, 76

Work values sorter, 70